THE BROKEN TRIANGLE

THE
BROKEN
TRIANGLE

Peking, Djakarta, and the PKI

Sheldon W. Simon

❋ ❋ ❋

The Johns Hopkins Press
Baltimore
Published in Cooperation with The Institute for
Sino-Soviet Studies, The George Washington University

To my Mother and Father

Preface

The Broken Triangle constitutes an analysis of a striking contemporary case of alliance formation in international politics between two radical-nationalist regimes—Communist China and Sukarno's Indonesia. It surveys the susceptibilities of elites in the two states to an informal alliance arrangement —the first between communist and noncommunist polities— and traces the construction of the alliance from the initial discovery of common goals, through the formation of the entente, to its ultimate destruction at the hands of a rival Indonesian elite. The study focuses on Chinese attempts to manipulate Indonesian politics through both Sukarno and his entourage as well as through the very important Indonesian Communist Party. Exploring the impact of the October 1965 abortive coup on the post-coup reciprocal perceptions of the two states, the study documents the precipitous shift in relations from cordiality to enmity in all issue-areas.

In order to place this extended case study in the cumulative literature on international politics, I have consciously set out my methodology and framework of analysis in the initial chapter, and I refer back to it periodically throughout the text. Those readers who are not interested in the concepts and methods of current international political analysis as such may wish to omit the first chapter and begin with the actual case analysis in Chapter Two. For those who, on the other hand, are concerned with methods of analysis as well as its substance, it is my hope that the first chapter will provide an analytical framework for the remainder of the manuscript.

I owe a considerable intellectual debt to a number of writers in the fields of Asian and international politics. I wish particularly to thank Professor Kurt London, director of the Institute for Sino-Soviet Studies at The George Washington University, for the grant which made the composition of this manuscript possible. I am also indebted to Professors Harold C. Hinton and Wolfgang Kraus of George Washington for their encouragement. An additional note of gratitude goes to the Kentucky Research Foundation for financial support in the preparation of the figures, charts, and tables in the manuscript.

Finally, I offer a special vote of thanks and affection to my wife, Charlann, who provided not only moral support and understanding for a hibernating scholar but also a first-born son just as the manuscript got under way. It is the author's sincere hope that his son will grow up to find China once more a productive and pacific major member of the international community. It is in this spirit that the following study is offered.

SHELDON W. SIMON

Lexington, Kentucky

Contents

List of Figures and Tables

THE BROKEN TRIANGLE

Introduction: International Political Theory and the Sino-Indonesian Case

Two parallel lines of inquiry have developed in the study of international politics in the last fifteen years. Each has produced important findings for both the academic and policy communities on a variety of international issues. Few proponents of either approach, however, have been willing to acknowledge the contributions of the other or the limitations of their own to an understanding of international politics. Instead, each tends to view the other as an opponent in a zero-sum game the goal of which is an "absolute truth," rather than as a partner with complementary skills in the quest for a cumulative political science where knowledge will grow, improve in scope, amount, and quality, and prove replicable for different analysts facing comparable problems. A number of labels have been given to these two research styles; perhaps the most accurate are *policy-analytical* and *empirical-theoretical*. These labels reflect both differing techniques and, for the most part, until recently, differing research problems. It is important to note, however, that both approaches are concerned with the real political world and differ only in the way in which they serve it.

Empirical-theorists have borrowed extensively from the

other social sciences in their quest for more incisive analytical tools. They have developed a variety of theories which, applied judiciously to political issues, have yielded significant insights. A partial listing of these theories would include conflict, bargaining, game theory, cybernetics, systems analysis, attitudes, and simulation.[1] The empirical-theorists maintain that the proliferation of applied social science concepts and methods has advanced the study of international politics by replacing the traditional few deterministic "causes" with a much larger number of significant variables held to interact in a probabilistic manner. As Karl Deutsch recently put it: "There has been an increase in the range, diversity, and effectiveness of empirical methods of investigation; an increase in the amounts, variety, and accuracy of quantitative data; and an increase in the breadth, versatility, and power of the available mathematical and statistical methods of data analysis and interpretation."[2] For the first time, the development of such multivariate analyses as factorization permits the political scientist to calculate the average contribution of each variable to the distribution of outcomes in a given case. Similarly, by applying different modes of analysis to the same issue, the political scientist can gather streams of evidence to buttress his interpretation. In the present study,

[1] Although this is not a bibliographic study, it is appropriate to list at least a few of the major sources in which empirical-theorists appear and in which a more extensive bibliography may be found. See, for example, J. David Singer's two works: *Human Behavior and International Politics: Contributions from the Social-Psychological Sciences* (Chicago: Rand McNally & Co., 1965) and *Quantitative International Politics* (New York: Free Press of Glencoe, 1968). See also the *Journal of Conflict Resolution* and the *Journal of Peace Research*. For one example of the use of content analysis and communications theory to analyze an international crisis, see Ole Holsti, Richard Brody, and Robert North, "Measuring Affect and Action in International Relations Models," *Journal of Peace Research* (1964): 3–4.

[2] Karl W. Deutsch, "Recent Trends in Research Methods in Political Science," in James C. Charlesworth, ed., *A Design for Political Science: Scope, Objectives, and Methods,* American Academy of Political and Social Sciences, Monograph no. 6 (Philadelphia, 1966), pp. 149–50. See also, Chadwick F. Alger, "Comparison of Intranational and International Politics," in R. Barry Farrell, ed., *Approaches to Comparative and International Politics* (Chicago: Northwestern University Press, 1966), p. 328.

for example, we shall be relying extensively on both qualitative content analysis of Chinese media and some semiquantitative analysis as well as system and communication theory, all of which can be checked against each other and against actual Chinese foreign policy behavior for either conflicting or supportive patterns. Thus, through the application of a variety of relevant techniques, trends may be identified which would not be apparent from imaginative speculation alone.[3]

The *policy-analyst* commenting on international politics tends to come from a different background. Generally, he is grounded in historical analysis and area studies and has devoted his research to the explanation of the politics and society of a given international region or country. His concern with specific policy problems renders his output of more immediate interest to the policy-maker than that of the empirical-theorist, who frequently focuses on the international system as a whole, oftentimes at such a high level of abstraction that the policy-maker does not perceive the research to be relevant to his concerns. As a prominent policy-analytical scholar on Chinese foreign affairs stated in the introduction to a recent book:

> I proceed on the basis of no general theory of social or political action; I find most such theories vague and pretentious. . . . I prefer history, in the sense of observed data and inferences from them to . . . the imposition of theory on data. This includes such skills as an understanding of what range of current meanings may be attached to familiar terminology, some appreciation of the limitations on the extent to which theory determines political action and a feeling for what has been omitted from a document as well as for what has been said. . . . If there is a master key, it is context and educated intuition.[4]

[3] Bruce M. Russett, "The Ecology of Future International Politics," *International Studies Quarterly*, 11, no. 1 (March, 1967): 14–15.
[4] Harold C. Hinton, *China in World Politics* (Boston: Houghton Mifflin Company, 1966), p. viii. A similar critique could be made of overgeneralizing from computer studies of international linkages. Brams, for example, found no

Although less universal than Hinton's criticism of empirical theory in international political research, Morton Kaplan quite accurately warns that the current level of theory development can generate only partial explanatory propositions and, indeed, may well be inapplicable to certain types of data and problems, such as foreign policy analysis: "This is an area in which extensive knowledge of a specific course of events, immense accumulation of detail, sensitivity and judgment in the selection of relevant factors, and intuitive ability of a high order are extremely important. We cannot easily use comparative evaluation, for the large number of variables involved in such events would not be even closely paralleled in other cases." [5]

Another analyst, employing the national-actor data collections of Russett/Alker and Banks/Textor to detect common patterns of behavior among states, similarly concludes that their predictive capabilities are "not sufficiently great to justify giving them priority over analyses . . . of the decision-making process." [6] Instead he suggests that analysts of Chinese affairs examine how Chinese policy-makers (a) articulate their values, (b) perceive the actions of other actors and adjust their own intentions, and (c) then translate these into policy.[7] While each of these caveats is well taken, it is of considerable importance to realize that in recent years some cross-fertilization on convergence between policy-analytical and empirical-

---

significant trade or diplomatic linkages between China and Indonesia in the mid-1960's. Yet, as we shall see, both states were engaged in a close foreign policy relationship. See S. J. Brams, "Transaction Flows in the International System, *American Political Science Review*, 60 (December, 1966): 4.

[5] Morton Kaplan, "The New Great Debate: Traditionalism vs. Science in International Relations," *World Politics*, 19, no. 1 (October, 1966): 11.

[6] Davis B. Bobrow, "Old Dragons in New Models," *World Politics*, 19, no. 2 (January, 1967): 310–11; and Thomas W. Robinson, "A National Interest Analysis of Sino-Soviet Relations," *International Studies Quarterly*, 11, no. 2 (June, 1967).

[7] Bobrow, "Old Dragons," p. 316, and David Vital, "On Approaches to the Study of International Relations, Or, Back to Machiavelli," *World Politics*, 19, no. 4 (July, 1967).

theoretical scholars has begun. On the one hand, representatives of the latter school have utilized historical and area specialists' data to develop general hypotheses;[8] on the other, area specialists have applied such general theories as personality and community integration to the regions they know best.[9]

It is my hope that this study will contribute to further convergence of area specialists and general theorists. The study follows the aphorism that methods and techniques are useful only insofar as they enable us to predict or explain phenomena with greater insight and accuracy. Pragmatism is the watchword: the employment of only those theories and techniques relevant to the data at hand. Thus quantitative content analysis, which will be used in the last part of this study, is only one technique for generating explanatory propositions on Chinese behavior; for quantification can only show us how *often* words, phrases, or themes recur in certain contexts, but it may miss entirely the meaning of a single sentence which gives an entirely new character to the document under analysis.[10] This is where the admonition of Hinton and Kaplan on the irrreplaceability of educated intuition becomes valuable. This does not invalidate the utility of the technique, however; rather, it should encourage the analyst to combine both *quantitative* and *qualitative* analysis—the former revealing a country's gross perceptions of the outside world, and the latter the salience and "meaning" of these perceptions for policy-makers.

[8] See, for example, Richard N. Rosecrance, *Action and Reaction in World Politics* (Boston: Little, Brown and Company, 1963); Arthur Banks and Robert Textor, *A Cross-Polity Survey* (Boston: M.I.T. Press, 1963); and the *Project Michelson Reports* (China Lake: Calif.).

[9] See Bernard K. Gordon, *The Dimensions of Conflict in Southeast Asia* (Englewood Cliffs, N.J.: Prentice-Hall, 1966), esp. chaps. 4 and 6; and Donald E. Weatherbee, *Ideology in Indonesia: Sukarno's Indonesian Revolution*, Southeast Asia Studies, no. 8 (New Haven: Yale University Press, 1966).

[10] Kenneth E. Boulding, "National Images and International Systems," *Journal of Conflict Resolution*, 7, no. 2 (June, 1959).

For the general theorist, the utility of this Sino-Indonesian study lies in the examination of a striking contemporary case of foreign policy change short of war—a change from coalition to enmity resulting from a shift in the position of domestic elites in one of the states. For the area specialist, the value of the study will lie in its examination of the evolution of reciprocal attitudes and policies of the principal actors (Sukarno and his associates, the Chinese People's Republic [CPR], and the Indonesian Communist Party [PKI]), beginning with the development of a confluence of domestic and foreign policy goals, on through the abrupt rupture of Gestapu and its aftermath of deteriorating relations, to the de facto Indonesian realignment.

Many of the questions raised during the course of our exploration are perceptual; for example, do the actors view the domestic and international environments in compatible ways when they are allies and in incompatible ways when they become antagonists? What impact do the confluence and the incompatibility of perceptions have on the actual formulation of policy? In effect, we shall be developing a discussion of influence in order to examine the impact the policies of one state have on susceptible elites in another, as well as attempting to assess the effect of internal political changes in one state on its relevant international environment. This is by no means an easy task; and such a method crosses the disciplinary boundaries of comparative and international politics.

For the student of national politics to concede that domestic processes may be significantly conditioned by foreign affairs is to run the risk of introducing a number of seemingly unpredictable factors into matters that he has become accustomed to taking for granted. Likewise, for the student of international politics to treat national phenomena as variables rather than constants is to invite a seemingly endless confounding of that which has otherwise proven manageable.[11]

Yet if we are to move beyond the conceptual confines of *national interest* as the only relevant factor in foreign policy analysis and beyond the notion of sovereignty in national politics to consider the fact that national boundaries are vulnerable to *informal penetration*, we must search for links to connect the differing units and settings of comparative and international politics.[12] And methods can be fruitful only when related to substantive problems.

One of the characteristics of international politics in the mid-twentieth century is *informal penetration,* a most useful concept for analyzing Sino-Indonesian affairs. Informal penetration refers to the ability of agents of one country to reach inside the boundaries of another to effect the former's interests. Informal penetration may be used to elicit cooperation as well as to promote conflict; it employs a wide variety of techniques, including propaganda, front groups, financial subsidization, militant party formation, strikes and riots, guerrilla warfare, and coups d'état.[13] "In a period of increasing informal access, a situation sometimes develops in which the critical boundary may not be the geographic one but one defined by the circumstances of the market, the location of adherents of an opposing ideology, the location of a given race or religious group or the zone of effectiveness of counterpenetration efforts." [14]

If we conceptualize the Sino-Indonesian relationship dur-

[11] James N. Rosenau, rapporteur, *Of Boundaries and Bridges: A Report on the Interdependence of National and International Political Systems* (Princeton: Center for International Studies, 1967), p. 5.

[12] *Ibid.,* pp. 8–9.

[13] Andrew M. Scott, *The Revolution in Statecraft: Informal Penetration* (New York: Random House, 1965), p. 4; James N. Rosenau, "Pre-theories and Theories of Foreign Policy," in Farrell, *Comparative and International Politics,* pp. 63–65; and Bruce Russett, *Trends in World Politics* (New York: Macmillan Company, 1965), p. 87.

[14] Scott, *Revolution in Statecraft,* p. 168.

ing the period of this study (1963–67) as both a traditional
state-to-state contact as well as one of Chinese informal penetration of Indonesia through a susceptible elite, like the PKI,
we can derive the following diagram.

MODEL OF CHINESE INFLUENCE IN INDONESIA

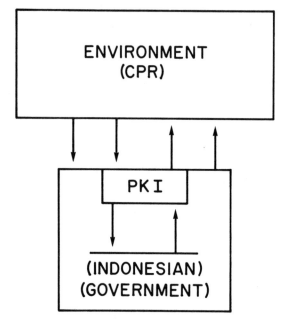

Groups other than the PKI would also be included. Cf. Robert T. Holt and
John E. Turner, "National-International Linkages—Geographic Conditions:
Insular Polities" (paper presented at the American Political Science Associa-
tion meeting, New York, 1966), pp. 6–7.

In addition, we can create a stimulus-response model to help explain information-processing and decision-making in the two states.

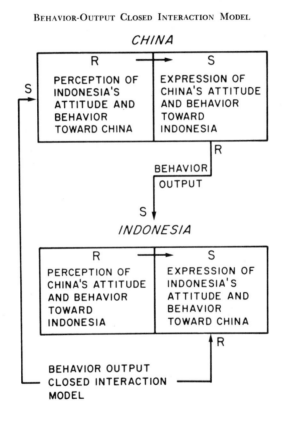

BEHAVIOR-OUTPUT CLOSED INTERACTION MODEL

Adapted from Ole Holsti, Richard Brody, and Robert North, "Measuring Affect and Action in International Relations Models," *Journal of Peace Research* (1964), p. 175.

It is useful to note for purposes of the study that S and R can be determined through propaganda content analysis. One could devise measurements for frequency and intensity as well as change over time by the simple equation: $PC = F_T \times I_T$, where PC means propaganda change, F_T means change in frequency over time, and I_T means change in intensity over time.[15]

Under Sukarno, Indonesia constituted a state which encouraged Chinese penetration and, for a period in 1965 before the attempted coup, almost permitted legitimacy to become attached to the direct participation of nonmembers of the state (CPR officials) in the allocation of Indonesia's values. The problem of assessing how this extraordinary relationship developed is one of the major tasks of this study.

Since the primary mode of analysis employed in this study is Sino-Indonesian reciprocal national perceptions with the greatest emphasis on Chinese perceptions, we must now explain the utility of content analysis in identifying these perceptions.

In a democratic-pluralistic political system, a major problem facing the analyst of national perceptions is the multiplicity of sources of viewpoints available and potentially relevant, including executive level statements, the official and nonofficial press, legislative reports, and positions emanating from that influential stratum—the "informed public." The problem of somehow weighing the impact of these various pressures on policy-makers is immense in a democratic system, but, fortunately, presents less difficulty for analysts of totalitarian states. Unlike pluralistic states where diffusion

---

[15] Once more it should be emphasized, however, that these techniques will provide only partial explanations. They can show us general trends in intensity and direction but cannot analyze subtleties of position. Only thematic textual analysis can do this. For a paper that falls into this trap, see Peter A. Toma, "Sociometric Measures of the Sino-Soviet Conflict: Peaceful and Nonpeaceful Revolutions" (paper presented at the American Political Science Association Meeting, New York, 1966).

characterizes information output, totalitarian states tend to coordinate their information activities, because mass media and "nongovernmental organizations" serve primarily as extensions of official policy. Thus, the analyst's task is simplified insofar as he can assume that *totalitarian mass media content contains the same perceptual qualities as those of the political leaders controlling the mass media.*

By employing a form of mass media thematic content analysis, one can attempt to assess the pattern of Peking's perception of any given foreign policy cluster—for our purposes Indonesia in particular and Southeast Asia in general.[16] By subjecting mass media output to systematic analysis, one can expect to determine which issues are salient to Chinese leaders and how they are perceived.

It seems that the Chinese are cognizant of the way in which outsiders analyze their media. Apparently to enhance communication, Peking has, in effect, established a *level of authoritativeness* to convey its own perceptions of the intensity and salience of a given issue to its various domestic and foreign audiences.

ROUGH RANK-ORDERING OF AUTHORITATIVENESS
OF CHINESE MEDIA LEVEL[17]

1. Official government statements.
2. "Commentator" and "Observer" articles in such papers as *People's Daily, Red Flag,* and *Liberation Army Daily.*
3. Editorials in the above papers.
4. Official and authorized New China News Agency (NCNA) statements.

---

[16] For a discussion of various types of *content analysis,* see Robert North, Ole Holsti, M. G. Zaninovich, and Dina Zinnes, *Content Analysis: A Handbook with Applications for the Study of International Crisis* (Evanston, Ill.: Northwestern University Press, 1963).

[17] For a complementary study on elite perception, see Henry G. Schwarz, "The Ts'an-K'ao Hsiao-hsi: How Well Informed Are Chinese Officials about the Outside World?" *China Quarterly* (September, 1966).

5. Statements of nongovernmental organizations, such as the China branch of the Afro-Asian People's Solidarity Organization (AAPSO).
6. Regular articles in the national press.
7. Regular NCNA "news reports."

Before attempting a thematic analysis of the available material, it is necessary to construct some appropriate categories in which to place the data. The author's own study of Chinese foreign policy as well as that of other analysts leads to the positing of three major overarching Chinese goals:[18] (*a*) recognition as a major world power, particularly since the initiation of its nuclear test series in 1964; (*b*) hegemony in Asia; and (*c*) leadership in the international communist movement.

In sum, I hope that the methods and concepts mentioned in this chapter as applied to contemporary Sino-Indonesian relations will enhance the exchange between the *policy-analytical* and the *empirical-theoretical* approaches. Social science research is confronted today with the problem of making its theoretical work relevant for policy analysts. In terms of the philosophy of science, this issue boils down to the problem of ideographic versus nomothetic knowledge, that is, the description of a particular situation on the one hand and the discovery of general laws on the other. At least the Sino-Indonesian case should be able to reveal some of the limitations as well as insights which general theories can produce when applied to specific cases.

[18] For some recent discussion of these goals, see Morton Halperin, *China and the Bomb* (New York: Frederick A. Praeger, 1965); Harold C. Hinton, "Sino-Soviet Rivalry in the Underdeveloped Areas." (Paper presented at the meeting of the Southern Political Science Association, November, 1966); and Sheldon Simon, "The Kashmir Dispute in Sino-Soviet Perspective," *Asian Survey* (March, 1967).

❖ 2

China and Indonesia: The Discovery of Common Goals

The development of a Sino-Indonesian entente was the result of an evolution in both regional and global international affairs whose beginning can be traced to the late 1950's. Its realization came about piecemeal as Peking perceived on the one hand favorable internal changes in Indonesia and on the other an increasingly hostile international environment elsewhere, including that within the international communist movement. Sukarno, for his part, after disposing of the Outer Islands Rebellion in 1959, similarly perceived the CPR as a potential ally for the realization of both his international and domestic policies. This chapter will attempt to delineate the commonly perceived interests which helped draw the two powers together.

Without delving into a history of China under the Mao regime, a discussion of some of the background factors which contribute to Peking's current foreign policy stances are in order. The atmosphere in which the current generation of Chinese Communist Party (CCP) leaders matured was one of national weakness, humiliation, and failure. It led to a disposition on the part of those leaders, once in power, to compensate for past failures not only by modernizing their country but also by working to eliminate Western influences from eastern Asia—the "rightful sphere of Chinese suzerainty." [1]

To accomplish these ends, the leadership had to develop a system for distinguishing allies from enemies. Based on their own *limited* experience in conflict against the Japanese, certain cognitive categories were developed and applied to international political data of the postwar world. These categories, based on the subjective past of the policy elites, helped them to define a limited number of roles for participants in a conflict and to generate expectations about the behavior of these role occupants. An examination of these roles reveals both the importance of the early Japanese experience to Chinese communist conflict theory and its resulting distortion of contemporary world politics. Important role categories included the *major enemy* and his *puppets* (in the context of the anti-Japanese war, the Japanese military and the Chinese who supported them). A category also existed for the phony ally (Chiang Kai-shek). Indicative of the Sino-centered nature of this system, no roles were provided for either the true ally or the true neutral. The latter, in effect, served the enemy by blurring the black-and-white distinction the party wished to present to the masses, while the former could only be a backer of China so long as it had no independent interests of its own. When independent interests developed, the state or group involved changed from backer to phony ally.[2] As we shall see, Peking viewed Sukarno's Indonesia as a backer rather than an ally, that is, a state whose articulated goals rendered it susceptible to Chinese leadership, not a partner in an independent bargaining position. This perceptual system is consistent with other

[1] Tang Tsou and Morton Halperin, "Mao Tse-tung's Revolutionary Strategy and Peking's International Behavior," *American Political Science Review,* 49 (March, 1965): 3.
[2] For an interesting discussion of the messianic political effects of these cognitive categories, see Davis B. Bobrow, "The Chinese Communist Conflict System," *Orbis,* 9 (Winter, 1966): 4.

content-analytic findings which suggest that Chinese elites "overperceive" the behavior of external actors in a negative direction, and that they perceive their own intentions toward others as highly correlated with their perception of the intentions of the others toward them.[3]

Thus, Chinese elites exclude from their circle of chosen friends any nationalist leaders, regardless of class origin, whom they do not consider to be struggling actively against imperialism, and include only those who oppose the West, even though they may be of royalist background. Peking's prognosis of favorable developments in these latter countries was spelled out in an October 1963 *Red Flag—People's Daily* editorial article contrasting the Chinese and Soviet positions in the underdeveloped world. The article predicted that internal crises would be accelerated in a country actively opposing imperialism, thus facilitating the rise to power of the local communist party in a period substantially shorter than that envisaged by Khrushchev. In addition, since the country would still be poor, it would presumably be more susceptible to Chinese guidance.[4] It may be more than coincidence that this editorial article appeared at the same time Peking began consolidating its relationship with Sukarno, and the Indonesian Communist Party (PKI) moved perceptibly toward Peking in the polemic.

By advocating both cooperation with anti-imperialist national leaders as well as local communist subversion, how-

---

[3] Bobrow, "Old Dragons," p. 316. A dramatic recent example of this perception of implacable external hostility is contained in a CPR Foreign Ministry Statement on the alleged espionage activities of an Indian diplomat in Peking who, the statement charged, was employed by "the imperialist, revisionist, and reactionary countries in China to engage unscrupulously in all kinds of illegal activities, trying to steal by every means political, military and economic intelligence about our country. . . ." (NCNA, June 14, 1967). Compare also Chinese charges against India and Indonesia in 1967 for conniving on attacks against Chinese diplomatic personnel, when this is precisely what the Chinese Government was doing in mass demonstrations against the embassies of these states.

[4] Cited in Hinton, *China in World Politics*, p. 72.

ever, Chinese leaders found themselves on the horns of a
dilemma in the underdeveloped world. This dilemma reflected the conflicting strains in China's own revolutionary
heritage (1937–45) between the necessity for a united front
against imperialism, on the one hand, and the experience of
betrayal by noncommunist elites which precluded total reliance on "revolution from above," on the other. For a time,
during the Bandung phase of its foreign policy (roughly
1954–58), Chinese leaders avoided the dilemma by not supporting the insurrectionary tactics of local revolutionaries in
exchange for commitments on the part of Asian governments
not to align with the United States. Peking offered a politico-
economic developmental model to these states, not so much
through foreign aid but rather by exporting doctrines of self-
reliance and state capitalism together with a form of virulent,
anti-imperialist nationalism.

Increasingly, however, the Chinese found their Asian policies in conflict with those of their major ally, the Soviet
Union. Sino-Soviet ideological tension, which characterized
the early years (1949–51) of CPR foreign policy, resurfaced
over the question of whether the CCP offered a unique
model for revolution in the developing world and whether
this model should be oriented primarily toward Asian governments or Asian communist parties. Although no clear-cut
abandonment of the former for the latter occurred, it became apparent in the late 1950's that China was devoting
more attention to "wars of national liberation" against incumbent governments than to its earlier strategy of cooperation with anti-imperialist bourgeois leaders. This change
came about as China perceived the disparity between the
underdeveloped world's interpretation of nonalignment and
its own. To the latter, nonalignment was *unidirectional*—
against the West; to the former, however, nonalignment became a strategy designed to elicit economic and political support from both blocs. Traumatized by the anti-Japanese/

anti-KMT period prior to their accession to power, Chinese decision-makers viewed this nonaligned strategy as the kind of betrayal that characterized the KMT in the 1940's, a betrayal which justified the abandonment of the united front policy.[5]

Nevertheless, *Pantjasila* and "the spirit of Bandung" were retained as communist shibboleths designed to give the CPR the best of both worlds: on the one hand, formally correct state-to-state relations, and on the other, no guarantee against Chinese pressures and interventions through party and overseas Chinese channels. In effect, the dilemma was avoided by adopting both strategies: overt appeals for unity with and encouragement of independent nationalist states and covert support for indigenous communist attacks upon the national-bourgeois governments. In other words, Peking was prepared to cooperate with noncommunist elites on anti-imperialist issues, but was not prepared to accept them as legitimate long-term leaders of their states. Instead, it insisted that Western pressures within the developing states would create social conditions conducive to the rise of local communist parties to power similar to those created by the Japanese occupation of China.[6]

The CCP counted on the attractiveness of its revolutionary doctrine of inevitable victory for indigenous leftist movements despite the absence of modern weapons and vast financial resources. In their place, the Chinese offered an expertise acquired through years of struggle and passed along through the training of new cadres—a more palatable alternative than the Soviet's appeal for communist cooperation with "national democratic states." In this doctrine, as elaborated most

[5] See the interesting Freudian interpretation of Maoist foreign policy in Richard H. Solomon, "Parochialism and Paradox in Sino-American Relations," *Asian Survey*, vol. 7, no 12 (December, 1967).

[6] Chalmers A. Johnson, "Building a Communist Nation in China," in Robert A. Scalapino, ed., *The Communist Revolution in Asia: Tactics, Goals, and Achievements* (Englewood Cliffs, N.J.: Prentice-Hall, 1965), p. 54.

recently by Lin Piao in September 1965, U.S. imperialism had come to occupy the special status of *major enemy;* for, Lin argued, America's role in Asia was analogous to the Japanese role in World War II. He concluded that neither a people's war nor *true* national independence could succeed without militant anti-Americanism. Peking was insisting, in effect, that the developing states adopt the CPR's world view as their own.

Peking's uncompromising ideology and revolutionary élan led in the post-Sputnik period to a falling-out with its then *major backer,* the U.S.S.R. When the U.S.S.R. refused to give military support to such important Chinese goals as the recovery of Taiwan and the consolidation of its Indian border region, the Sino-Soviet rift appeared. As it has developed in the last ten years, the bitterness of this rift reflects not only the fact that each contender has come to pursue conflicting foreign policy goals but also that each views the other as a heretic to Marxism-Leninism. Thus, the conflict has pervaded both state and party relations as each side tries to outmaneuver the other in relations with the rest of the socialist camp, among the nonaligned states, and within the communist parties in noncommunist states. As a Soviet commentator put it exasperatedly: "The Mao Tse-tung group uses China's trade and economic relations with Afro-Asian countries to separate them from the socialist community, to create obstacles for and even undermine economic cooperation between socialist and Afro-Asian states. The aim of Chinese policy is to create an exclusive bloc, a sort of Afro-Asian community in which China plays the main role." [7]

By the late 1950's, Peking found itself on the short end of the disintegrating Sino-Soviet alliance, losing both economic and military aid as well as diplomatic support within the international communist movement. By virtue of its greater

---

[7] G. Apalin, "Peking's Policy in Africa and Asia," *Africa and Asia Today,* summarized by *Tass,* September 29, 1967.

aid capacity, Moscow was even able to isolate the Chinese in such Asian front groups as the Afro-Asian Solidarity Secretariat.[8]

As Chinese leaders began to question the viability of their old alliance with the Soviets, a potential new ally emerged on the scene. By 1961, Sukarno had managed to acquire virtual dictatorial powers in Indonesia through discrediting and/or incarcerating his moderate opposition. In the process, he advanced the prospects of the PKI which by this time had penetrated the largest political party in the country, the Indonesian Nationalist Party (PNI). While the Chinese were aware of these developments in Indonesia, it seems probable that their first specific realization of the potentialities of an Indonesian alliance did not occur until Sukarno's address to the 1961 Belgrade conference where, in effect, he echoed the Chinese interpretation of world affairs.[9] Indonesia followed this initial performance by serving as Peking's spokesman at the Colombo Conference on Sino-Indian border hostilities. Sukarno appeared not merely to be enamored of Marxism in general, but of the Maoist variant in particular, which maintained that developing countries could skip certain stages and move directly into socialism.[10]

In any case, by January 1963, a certain amount of Sino-Indonesian foreign policy coordination became apparent. Both Sukarno and the Maoist regime were seeking a more radical alignment in world affairs than was offered by either the old nonaligned grouping or the Europe-centered socialist group. Indeed, in a letter to the Italian communist party leader Togliatti, in October, Peking in effect accused the Soviet Union of being unable to understand the national liberation

[8] Franz Michael, "Communist China and the Noncommitted Countries," in *New Nations in a Divided World*, ed. Kurt London (New York: Frederick A. Praeger, 1963), p. 249.
[9] See Chen I's statement in *Peking Review*, 14 (April 5, 1963): 6.
[10] Ernst Kux, "Communist Tactics in Nonaligned Countries and the Ideological Quarrel Between Moscow and Peking," in London, *New Nations*, p. 262.

struggle of the Afro-Asian states because of Russia's European background.[11] Initially the Afro-Asian conference seemed to be an appropriate vehicle to both states. Thus, Chou Enlai was quick to offer warm Chinese support for the Indonesian-initiated proposal for a second conference.[12] Following up the Indonesian proposal, Chou made a tour of ten African countries (December 1963–February 1964), in the course of which he sought to convince these states to give priority to another Afro-Asian meeting over a second nonaligned conference where such Chinese antagonists as Yugoslavia and India would be represented.

The point of Sino-Soviet no-return was reached with the conclusion of the partial nuclear test-ban treaty in the summer of 1963. In September, Peking and Djakarta began operating in tandem within the Afro-Asian movement to wrest control away from the Soviets. At the September AAPSO conference in Nicosia, the two delegations pressed for a new Afro-Asian labor conference from which the U.S.S.R. would be excluded. Following this proposal, a whole series of conferences, which usually spawned permanent secretariats, were planned for Djakarta in the fields of labor, journalists', student, artists', women's and seamen's affairs.[13] The inevitable and predictable joint communiqués of these meetings all carried the Peking-Djakarta combined line of militant hostility to the West with encouragement to "national liberation struggles" throughout the underdeveloped world.

In this early period of collaboration (1961–63), Peking perceived and employed Indonesia as its noncommunist entrée into the Afro-Asian world. By 1963, this relationship became

---

[11] Cited in V. P. Dutt, "China and Southeast Asia," in *Japan's Future in Southeast Asia*, Center for Southeast Asian Studies (Kyoto, 1966), p. 97.

[12] NCNA, January 2, 1963.

[13] Justus M. Van der Kroef, "The Sino-Indonesian Partnership," *Orbis*, 8, no 2 (Summer, 1964): 352; and Michael Freeberne, "Racial Issues and the Sino-Soviet Dispute," *Asian Survey*, 5 (August, 1965): 8.

a part of the CPR's strategy to break out of the isolated position within the international communist movement into which the U.S.S.R. had maneuvered it after the Partial Nuclear Test-Ban Treaty. Indonesia could serve as China's "backer," while vocal Chinese support first for Indonesia's recovery of West Irian and subsequently for Djakarta's *Konfrontasi* ("confrontation") policy against Malaysia had the effect of showing Indonesian leaders that they possessed a "powerful" Asian ally who could facilitate Djakarta's foreign policy by substituting links with the Asian socialist camp for Western ties.[14]

INDONESIA'S SUSCEPTIBILITY TO A CHINESE CLIENT RELATIONSHIP

The dynamics of Sino-Indonesian alliance formation may best be understood by an examination of the predispositions of policy elites in the two states toward cooperation. These predispositions ranged from the supposed ideological consonance of the Chinese and Indonesian revolutions to such pragmatic calculations as the best method for organizing Afro-Asian front groups to eliminate the influence of such moderates as India. In Indonesia they also included the uneasy cooperation of such strange bedfellows as the opportunists around Sukarno—the army and the PKI—each for its own domestic political strategies.

---

[14] For a PKI endorsement of this development, see D. N. Aidit, *Set Afire the "Banteng" Spirit! Ever Forward, No Retreat!* Report to the Second Plenum of Seventh PKI Central Committee, December 23–26, 1963. (Peking: Foreign Languages Press, 1964), pp. 52–59. See also Hinton, *China in World Politics,* pp. 169–70. Further evidence of the differences between the CPR and U.S.S.R. as early as 1961 on the role the socialist camp should play in the underdeveloped world is available in a computerized content analysis of Chinese and Soviet foreign policy statements in which the CPR scored several points higher on scales of frustration, hostility, and desire to change the status quo. See Robert North, "Two Revolutionary Models: Russian and Chinese," in A. Doak Barnett, *Communist Strategies in Asia* (Frederick A. Praeger, 1963), pp. 54, 59, 60.

Under the impact of Sukarno's personality Indonesian politics between 1960 and 1965 took on a heavily *ideosyncratic* hue, that is, reflective of Sukarno's particular ideology and world view. Ideology's political function is the provision of legitimation, particularly for authoritarian regimes for which there may be few other bases for consensus. Ideology defines, orders, and tests the political present and prescribes courses of action for the future.

Sukarno's rise to preeminence in Indonesian politics in the late 1950's led to a shift in the country's ideological and, ultimately, international political orientation. Sukarno viewed with suspicion, if not outright hostility, the substitution of economic and social progress—as urged by the West—for the destruction of an alien enemy (as touted by Mao's national liberation notions). In other words, Sukarno felt threatened by the application of objective achievement criteria as a test of his regime's success. Reliance on charisma, by contrast, permitted him to define his own standards of revolution and use them to appeal to an undifferentiated public for support. The key to understanding the impact of Sukarno's thought on Indonesian foreign policy lay in his ability to intertwine domestic and foreign affairs so that success in one realm could occur only with comparable success in the other: "The Indonesian Revolution and the revolution of Asia and Africa are to uproot imperialism, to uproot colonialism, to uproot capitalism, in order to build socialism, to consolidate a new world." [15]

Because of his key position in the political structure, Sukarno was able to project his ideology onto the nation at large—an ideology involving highly affective symbols oriented toward a hostile outgroup and so abstract that any real

[15] Sukarno, April 11, 1965, to MPRS, cited in Donald E. Weatherbee, *Ideology in Indonesia: Sukarno's Indonesian Revolution,* Southeast Asia Monograph Series, no. 8 (New Haven: Yale University Press, 1966), p. 25.

information content was minimal.[16] The gist of Sukarno's world view by 1961, which we shall see was quite compatible with Peking's, was that the era of bipolar neutralism when nonaligned states could mediate between the superpowers had been completed. Instead a new world power distribution was developing, based on the concept he had introduced at the Belgrade conference: the New Emerging Forces (NEFO) versus the Old Established Forces (OLDEFO).[17]

Earlier, Sukarno had espoused a moderate nonaligned policy epitomized by the 1955 *Pantjasila* of Bandung fame. Along with Nehru, he had focused his attentions on disarmament and nuclear testing. Sukarno's decision to turn to the West Irian issue in 1960, however, marked a watershed in Indonesian foreign policy as evidenced by the change in tone and theme of his foreign affairs remarks. The Indonesian president soft-pedaled his references to nonalignment and the bipolar conflict and began to speak of the necessity for a "third force" in international politics. He dwelt on Indonesia's mission as a world power and, upon return from a visit to Eastern Europe, claimed foreign admiration for his notions of "Guided Democracy." Sukarno capped these developments by delivering a fiery address to the U.N. General Assembly in the autumn of 1960 which appeared to be a virtual declaration of war on the capitalist West as well as an appeal for leadership among the new states. The Bung's success in gaining West Irian the following year seemed to reinforce his conviction that there existed an irreconcilable NEFO-OLDEFO struggle in which peace must yield priority to "liberation."

[16] For a discussion of the impact of such a charismatic type, see Sidney Verba, "Assumptions of Rationality and Non-Rationality in Models of the International System," in *The International System: Theoretical Essays*, ed. Klaus Knorr and Sidney Verba (Princeton: Princeton University Press, 1962), pp. 103–4.

[17] Masataka Kosaka, "Characteristics of International Relations in Southeast Asia," in Center for Southeast Asian Studies, *Japan's Future*, pp. 84–85.

Indonesian foreign policy had become an extension of Sukarno's domestic revolutionary process. Thus, just as there
were OLDEFO forces to destroy internally, such as Masjumi
and the PSI, so there were OLDEFO forces in the international realm which must be eliminated in order to overthrow
the few exploiters (read: Western states) of subjected nations
(read: Afro-Asian states). Although coexistence might be possible in the bipolar context, to Sukarno it was unacceptable
as a general rule of international conduct, particularly between the NEFO and the OLDEFO. Rather, as we shall see,
his hope was to forge a new group of allies, selectively drawn
from the socialist and nonaligned camps, who would support
such Indonesian goals as *Konfrontasi* and cater to Sukarno's
egomania for a major voice in international councils. Any
teeth in his erstwhile alliance would come through Chinese
military strength which, in combination with other Asian
communist states and Indonesia, would cooperate to expel
Western influence and alter the regional status quo.

In effect, this became a bid by Sukarno to ally with the
evolving Peking wing of the bloc, particularly since he frequently reiterated that the aim of the Indonesian revolution
was also the creation of a "socialist society." Paralleling this
bid for new international alignment was the politicization
of nongovernmental groups and activities within Indonesia,
which emphasized ideological obedience to Sukarno's variant
of Marxism-Leninism.[18] It is not likely that the compatibility
of Sukarnoism and Maoism was missed by the Chinese.[19] Certainly the PKI had many opportunities to present its case for
cooperation with Sukarno to the Chinese party. In addition,
the Indonesian archipelago had been of strategic interest to

---

[18] Weatherbee, *Ideology in Indonesia*, p. 46.
[19] Stuart Schram, "Chinese and Leninist Components in the Personality of
Mao Tse-tung," *Asian Survey*, 2 (June, 1963): 6. Also, Justus M. Van der Kroef,
"An Indonesian Ideological Lexicon," *Asian Survey*, vol. 1, no. 7 (July, 1962).

the Chinese even before Mao's rise to power. Sun, for example, spoke of it as a former area of Chinese control.[20]

Groundwork had been laid for a potential Peking–Djakarta relationship from China's standpoint as far back as 1956 when Sukarno made his first visit to the Chinese capital. At that time, Chinese leaders and the Peking press hailed his arrival as "an event of paramount importance . . . which confirms completely the present and long-term interests of both our peoples." On his return to Djakarta, Sukarno cited China as a "model" for Indonesia's "new style democracy." [21]

Paradoxically, Indonesia's recovery of West Irian, thanks to U.S. diplomatic pressure, was interpreted by both Sukarno and Peking as justification for the efficacy of the former's radicalism. Even African opposition to Sukarno's West Irian claim in the United Nations served only to convince him of the need of replacing his ties with the moderates in international relations by an alliance with Peking.[22] As Brackman put it: "Although Indonesia was wholly dependent on foreign arsenals and silos for arms and food, Sukarno and his aides were so intoxicated with their 'conquests' they began seriously to believe that Indonesia had attained 'great power status' and, therefore, was entitled to a sphere of influence in Southeast Asia." [23]

To the Chinese, an Indonesian sphere of influence in the island archipelago appeared a not unwelcome prospect as both sides increasingly appeared to share such strategic goals as: (a) discrediting the United States and United Kingdom positions in Southeast Asia; (b) the fragmentation of Malay-

[20] Cited in Robert North, *Chinese Communism* (New York: McGraw-Hill, 1966), p. 87.
[21] Cited in Arnold Brackman, "The Malay World and China," in *Policies Toward China: Views from Six Continents*, ed. A. M. Halpern (New York: McGraw-Hill, 1965), p. 274.
[22] Arnold Brackman, *Southeast Asia's Second Front* (New York: Frederick A. Praeger, 1966), p. 110.
[23] *Ibid.*, p. 114.

sia; (c) the elimination of anti-leftist movements in Indonesia; and (d) the division of Southeast Asia into separate
spheres of influence for Peking, Hanoi, and Djakarta.[24]

Perhaps with these goals in mind, the Indonesian chargé in
Peking in April 1963 expressed Sukarno's admiration for
China's example in world affairs: "A powerful China has
brought great stability to Asia and the whole world . . . and
raised the prestige of the newly independent countries which
were once colonies." [25]

Liu Shao-chi's visit to Indonesia the same month served to
continue this warm relationship by making the "first trip
ever made by China's head of state to friendly Asian countries" an "event of major political significance." After praising Indonesia's "glorious revolutionary tradition," Liu "emphasized that Indonesia is playing an ever more important
role in international affairs, and its international status is
continuously rising." Liu outlined a number of common interests of the two states, mentioning Sukarno's 1961 performance at Belgrade, his proposal for a second Afro-Asian
conference and the Games of the New Emerging Forces
(GANEFO) which "reflects the strong desire of the Asian and
African peoples to free themselves from imperialist manipu-
lation in international organizations," and the "just stand"
of opposing "the neocolonialist scheme of Malaysia and supporting the revolutionary struggle of the people of North
Kalimantan." Liu appeared fully to accept Indonesia as an
ally when he stated: "The Republic of Indonesia has become
an important force opposing imperialism and colonialism
and safeguarding the peace and security of Southeast Asia and
Asia as a whole." [26] Two weeks later, in summing up Liu's
visit, the *Peking Review* declared: "The strengthening of the

[24] For some insightful discussions, see J. O. Sutter, "Two Faces of 'Konfrontasi': Crush Malaysia and the 'Gestapu,' " *Asian Survey*, 6 (October, 1966): 531–
32; Gordon, *Conflict in Southeast Asia*, pp. 80–119.
[25] *Peking Review*, 14 (April 5, 1963): 6.
[26] *Peking Review*, 16 (April 19, 1963): 7–9.

unity and cooperation between the two great Asian nations, which together represent one-fourth of the world's population, will substantially augment the forces defending Asian and world peace." Agreeing with Sukarno's appeal for NEFO unity, Liu defined the Chinese conception of this grouping as "the forces of world socialism and the national democratic movement." [27] Peking followed its words of support with deeds so that by the time of the abortive coup in October 1965 (in just three years) Indonesia had become China's largest economic aid recipient.[28]

The development by two states such as China and Indonesia of common world views enhances the prospect for a potential alliance through the process of "selective memory," that is, endemic antagonisms are played down by each side to decrease sources of strain. Both Peking's and Djakarta's treatment of the periodic anti-Chinese repressions in Indonesia is illustrative of this principle. As early as 1959, Sukarno appeared cognizant of possible future benefits in a pro-China policy, but he was not yet so closely tied to Peking that he was willing to risk domestic political costs. Thus, when anti-overseas-Chinese riots occurred, the Indonesian government declared: "We shall, under all circumstances, maintain friendship with the People's Republic of China *but without sacrificing our national interests.*" (Emphasis added.) [29] Even the conclusion of a Dual Nationality Treaty in 1960 did not visibly ameliorate economic discrimination against the Overseas Chinese, although it provided a way for the CPR to extricate itself from the impossible job of trying to protect their interests. Sukarno's efforts to liberalize the conditions under which Indonesian citizenship could be obtained were gratefully acknowledged by Chen I in his March 1961 visit to

[27] *Peking Review*, 18 (May 3, 1963): 10.
[28] P. A. Poole, "Communist China's Aid Diplomacy," *Asian Survey*, 6, no. 11 (November, 1966): 626.
[29] Cited in Brackman, "The Malay World and China," p. 279.

Djakarta, during the course of which a new Friendship Treaty was signed.

By May 1963, the Sino-Indonesian relationship had become much closer, particularly after Liu Shao-chi's April visit, in which a diplomatic alliance was all but formally proclaimed. When anti-Chinese violence recurred in Bandung, resulting in a number of Chinese casualties and several million dollars of property damage, Sukarno, whose past explanations had indirectly accused Chinese residents of economic exploitation, changed his tack by charging that the riots were engineered by "counterrevolutionaries at home as well as by foreign subversives" who, seeking to topple his government, had chosen the Chinese minority "because we have lately been in close contact with People's China." [30] Peking accepted this explanation and praised Sukarno for taking appropriate measures to restore order.[31] The conscious decision of the two states to minimize the ethnic strain of the Indonesian Chinese community during the alliance period presents a dramatic contrast to both the Indonesian treatment of resident Chinese after the coup attempt and the Chinese reaction to this treatment.

By the time of Indonesia's inauguration of *Konfrontasi* in September 1963, Peking seemed quite satisfied with both foreign and domestic policy developments in Djakarta. Since late 1961, Indonesia had gratuitously made a number of moves which could only be construed as the representation of China's interests by proxy. In 1962, for example, Djakarta refused Taiwan admission to the Asian Games, an act which Peking gratefully acknowledged: "The Chinese people, sportsmen, and all those connected with athletics wished to express their deep gratitude to President Sukarno and the Indonesian Government and people for their unflinching

---

[30] Cited in Van der Kroef, "The Sino-Indonesian Partnership," *Orbis*, 8, no. 2 (Summer, 1964): 333.
[31] See the *Peking Review*, 21 (May 24, 1963): 20.

stand to safeguard Afro-Asia solidarity and Sino-Indonesian friendship." [32]

Indonesian foreign minister Subandrio represented Peking's position at the Colombo conference on Sino-Indian border hostilities and this too was acknowledged by the CPR during his January 1963 visit to Peking.[33]

During this whole period of Indonesian pre-alliance activity, Peking reciprocated by providing strong propaganda support to Indonesia for its "recovery" of West Irian, implicitly derogating the temporary U.N. administration. In a speech during Subandrio's visit, Chou En-lai insisted on the necessity of sustaining the struggle for West Irian despite U.N. promises, and indirectly cautioned the Indonesian foreign minister about the plebiscite provision: ". . . the imperialists are not reconciled to abandoning their colonial interests, they are still creating all sorts of pretexts for hanging on in West Irian." Thus, "it is also necessary to wage a struggle in order to *compel* the imperialists to observe an agreement." (Emphasis added.)[34]

By mid-1963, then, Peking and Djakarta each saw the opportunity to exploit a useful alliance with the other. Peking already possessed evidence of Sukarno's willingness to represent China to the Afro-Asian world, even on such unpopular issues as the Sino-Indian border war and the Asian Games. For its part, Djakarta viewed the CPR as a keystone of its NEFO concept and an ally against the West in international affairs, as well as a potential model for domestic emulation as Sukarno acted to restructure Indonesian politics toward his own variant of Marxism-Maoism.

---

[32] *Peking Review,* 1 (September 7, 1962): 17.

[33] *Ibid.* (January 4, 1963): 23.

[34] *Ibid.* For a somewhat different interpretation of Chinas interest in moderating any full-scale Indonesian military campaign in West Irian because of its potential enhancement of Soviet military influences, see Hinton, *China in World Politics,* p. 434.

3

The Sino-Indonesian Alliance
Part One: *Konfrontasi* and the Division of Asia

Indonesia's decision to "confront" Malaysia provided the mortar necessary to cement the Sino-Indonesian relationship. Whereas earlier examples of cooperation were unilateral and gratuitous, for example, Indonesia's enunciation of Chinese policy at international conferences from which Peking was excluded, *Konfrontasi* proved to be an issue which entailed persistent diplomatic and material support from Peking to Djakarta.

For Indonesian domestic politics, this new adventure accelerated Sukarno's program of creating the trappings of a totalitarian state while eliciting support from the two major actors in national affairs—the military and the PKI. Sukarno paid a price for this policy, however, for by stifling opposition and discouraging disinterested intelligence-gathering, his own decision-makers received an increasingly distorted picture of the real world that led over time to a considerable gap between Indonesia's actual capability in Southeast Asia and its self-delusion of major power status. For Sukarno, during the course of *Konfrontasi*: "Patriotism consists in reacting favorably to a monolithic system of propaganda. . . . External debate is confined as far as pos-

sible to narrowly circumscribed areas of subject matter. . . .
The system, to a very considerable extent, denies foreign
policy leadership the benefits which may be gained from
internal nongovernmental criticism and the identification
of policy alternatives. . . . [all these] combine to make
judgement about popular opposition and support both difficult and uncertain." [1]

As Sukarno's foreign policy establishment increasingly restricted its information input to him, including only reports
of alleged Indonesian successes in international affairs and
ascribing hostile actions exclusively to the "enemy," Indonesia's external and internal behavior began to fit the psychoanalytic concepts of *projection* and *introjection*. In the
former, a quality is attributed to an external object (Malaysia) which is in fact characteristic of the attributor (aggressive expression). Thus, the latter can act without international guilt feelings. Introjection applies when representatives
of the enemy are perceived as being present within the
country. Thus, opposition can be equated with treason and
effectively stifled.[2] To Sukarno and his aides, then, Malaysia
appeared as a new Western arrangement to maintain British
interests in Southeast Asia. Because of their own experiences, they could not visualize a free association between an
emergent Asian state and a Western power. Their world
was composed of extremes: either total alliance as with the
CPR and NEFO or total opposition against the "neocolonial-
ists" behind Malaysia who were bent on encircling and
destroying Indonesia.[3]

As early as 1945, Sukarno had stated his views on Indo-

---

[1] R. Berry Farrell, "Foreign Policies of Open and Closed Societies," in *Approaches to Comparative and International Politics,* ed. R. Berry Farrell
(Evanston: Northwestern University Press, 1966), p. 194.

[2] For a discussion of the use of psychoanalytic categories to explain international politics, see James N. Rosenau, rapporteur, *Boundaries and Bridges*
(Princeton: Center for International Studies, 1967), pp. 34–45.

[3] Arnold Brackman, *Southeast Asia's Second Front* (New York, Frederick A.
Praeger, 1966), pp. 154–88.

nesian hegemony in the archipelago: "Indonesia will not become strong and secure unless the whole Straits of Malacca is in our hands." [4] Such an early policy led to the development of norms of international conduct by Sukarno's regime different from those held by the West and compatible with the Chinese Communist system. Thus, Indonesia not only had the right but also the obligation to interfere in the affairs of its neighbors to achieve its goals. Such interference was not just surreptitious but often quite overt and unashamed. And despite internal mutual hostility, both the PKI and the military agreed on the correctness of Sukarno's view.

For both Indonesia and China, the prelude to the "Crush Malaysia" campaign occurred with the Brunei revolt in December 1962. To Sukarno this unsuccessful uprising "proved" that the whole Malaysia project was unstable because, he concluded, it did not possess the support of the people of Borneo. The Manila conference of the following August probably reinforced this notion as Sukarno emerged with the impression that both Macapagal and Rahman basically agreed with his assessment which was embodied in the joint statement of the conference that foreign military bases were temporary and that none of the signatories would allow "arrangements of collective defense to serve the particular interests of any of the big powers." [5] Sukarno and Subandrio saw any prospective MAPHILINDO not as an enterprise for regional cooperation but as a device to obstruct the formation of Malaysia. Malaysia's fragmentation would have been perfectly acceptable to Indonesia since the resultant small states would probably evolve into Indonesian satellites.

Peking's opportunistic support of the Brunei uprising re-

[4] Cited in Bernard K. Gordon, *Dimensions of Conflict in Southeast Asia* (Englewood Cliffs, N.J.: Prentice-Hall, 1966), p. 93.
[5] *Ibid.*, p. 102.

flected not her enthusiasm for Azahari's band but rather her desire to jump on the Indonesian bandwagon. Virtually all Chinese statements on Brunei were made in the context of broader Sino-Indonesian relations.[6] Indeed, by supporting Azahari, Peking seemed to be undercutting its own client party, the Clandestine Communist Organization (CCO) in Sarawak. A victory for Azahari would have meant that instead of domination by Kuala Lumpur, British Borneo would have been controlled by the hereditary sultanate of Brunei, hardly an acceptable alternative to the CCO. In fact, not a single Chinese was implicated in the Azahari uprising.[7] Nonetheless, Peking, Djakarta, and the PKI all hailed the Brunei example as the "way to liberation" for Malaysia's component parts.

The Brunei revolt proved a windfall for Sukarno. It offered a new adventure after the settlement of Irian and provided a new antagonist in the British. Until then, popular interest in Malaysia had been noticeably lacking in Indonesia. The uprising countered this lack of enthusiasm as Indonesian media depicted it not as an isolated development in a tiny sultanate but rather as a revolution which engulfed Sarawak and Sabah as well, a position also held by Peking. On February 14, 1963, after earlier joint pronouncements on Brunei by Subandrio and the Chinese, Sukarno formally declared Indonesia's opposition to the Malaysian scheme. In March, Peking expressed the conviction that with Sino-Indonesian assistance, the Brunei rebels "will certainly be able to win final victory." Throughout 1963, Afro-Asian communist front groups on which

---

[6] Justus M. Van der Kroef, "The Sino-Indonesian Partnership," *Orbis*, 8, no. 2 (Summer, 1964): 342.

[7] For an enlightening discussion of the respective relations of Peking, Djakarta, and the CCO with Azahari, see Francis L. Starner, "Communism in Malaysia: A Multifront Struggle," in *The Communist Revolution in Asia*, ed. Robert Scalapino (Englewood Cliffs, N.J.: Prentice-Hall, 1965), and Brackman, *Southeast Asia's Second Front*, p. 142.

Indonesia and the CPR were represented echoed their denunciations of Malaysia and proffered support for an independent North Kalimantan.[8]

For the PKI, joint Chinese-Indonesian support for Azahari and subsequent opposition to Malaysia vindicated its own policy which dated back to 1961, even prior to the West Irian settlement. First in a *Harian Rakjat* editorial of August 31 and then at the party plenum in December, the PKI dubbed Malaysia a new form of neocolonialism. Support was urged for organized resistance by the peoples of the territories, and the PKI, in hopes of aborting the embryonic union, initiated its own aid program to remnants of the Malayan Communist Party (MCP), the Barisan Sosialis, and the CCO.[9]

Confrontation served the PKI cause of keeping the military occupied on the border, rather than hunting down party operatives in Central and East Java and Sumatra. It also placed the party in the forefront of Indonesian politics as both Sukarno and the military appeared to be following the PKI's lead. Speaking to the central committee plenum in December 1963, however, Aidit displayed some concern that the Malaysia campaign would be used as an excuse to delay domestic political and economic reforms, particularly the revocation of the State of Emergency which gave the military civilian police power in much of the country.

For the military, confrontation permitted the maintenance of an overinflated budget and also served to obstruct Chinese influence in the archipelago. The military perceived Malaysia to be dominated by the Chinese of Singapore, despite the

[8] D. N. Aidit, *Dare, Dare and Dare Again!* Political Report to First Plenary Session of Seventh PKI Central Committee, February 10, 1963 (Peking: Foreign Languages Press, 1963), p. 58; Brackman, *Southeast Asia's Second Front,* pp. 147, 149–50; and "Uprising in Brunei," *Peking Review,* vol. 50 (December 21, 1963).
[9] J. O. Sutter, "Two Faces of 'Konfrontasi',", pp. 535–37, and Van der Kroef, "The Sino-Indonesian Partnership," p. 335.

fact that one of the purposes of the union was to dilute the radical Chinese left in Singapore and provide a more economically viable state for the Chinese, Malays and Indians. Finally, the military also shared Sukarno's vision of a hegemonic Indonesia. In January 1964, General Yani, chief-of-staff, announced that Indonesia's security policy was changing from "a defense concept based on her own national territory" to one which included an "international element in the form of this country's responsibility and contribution toward security and stability in Southeast Asia." [10]

Beginning in January 1963, during Sukarno's visit to China, both Peking and Djakarta launched a cooperative propaganda campaign of support for Azahari's "national liberation movement," although neither state was prepared at this time to permit him to set up a government-in-exile. Opposition to Malaysia and support for North Borneo's independence became for Peking a new test case of ideological and tactical differences with the U.S.S.R. The fact that communist guerrillas from Sarawak were being trained by the Indonesian Army in Indonesian Borneo in September 1963 and that with Sukarno's apparent blessing the CCO and PKI were in direct communication by 1962 served to convince Peking even more that Indonesia was a worthwhile backer in the national liberation struggle.[11] In December 1963 the Chinese indicated the importance they attached to protracted struggle in North Borneo by hailing it as "a component part of the liberation fight in Southeast Asia." [12]

With the development of the Malaysian confrontation, Indonesian leaders may well have calculated that they had

---

[10] For an excellent refutation of Indonesian logic on the political role of Singapore Chinese, see Brackman, *Southeast Asia's Second Front*, pp. 3–54. For the Indonesian military's reevaluation of foreign policy, see Justus Van der Kroef, "Exporting Indonesia's Revolution," *Eastern World*, 18 (July, 1964): 14.

[11] Van der Kroef, "The Sino-Indonesian Partnership," p. 343; and Brackman, *Southeast Asia's Second Front*, p. 64.

[12] *Peking Review*, vol. 51 (December 20, 1963).

acquired the best of two worlds. On the one hand, as the result of the de facto alliance with China, Indonesia was provided with diplomatic, propaganda, and aid resources to press its claims on neighboring states; and on the other, Indonesia felt no qualms about the possible adverse effects of Chinese power on itself, since the U.S. Seventh Fleet was interposed between the two states. Besides, Peking had apparently excluded Indonesia per se from its list of "lost territories." [13] Sukarno was aware, however, of the fact that the Seventh Fleet was a two-edged sword. It could also obstruct an Indonesian invasion of the Malay peninsula, as it earlier had deterred a direct invasion of Irian. It is interesting to speculate that during his June 1961 visit to Peking, the Indonesian president may have encouraged the CPR to undertake a diversionary action in the Taiwan Strait in order to give Indonesia the necessary leeway to launch its own Irian expedition. China's refusal at that time may well have led to Indonesia's tactical shift in mid-1961 away from preparation for a full-scale assault on West Irian to small-scale infiltration instead, a tactic which it repeated in Malaysia during the course of *Konfrontasi*.[14]

The Malaysian Confrontation: Sino-Indonesian Euphoria

Malaysia's decision to try to negotiate an end to Indonesia's confrontation proved to be a tactical error, because Sukarno did not seek an end to the crisis as such. He wanted either to prolong it for such internal political reasons as the radicalization of the country or to bring about the total dissolution of the federation. For Sukarno, the game of *Konfrontasi* was "zero-sum." Indonesia's behavior at the several confer-

[13] In 1954 the CPR published a map showing its lost territories, which included Singapore and Malaysia but excluded Indonesia. See Brackman, *Southeast Asia's Second Front*, p. 8.
[14] See the suggestive discussion in Hinton, *China in World Politics*, pp. 434–35.

ences dealing with Malaysia in Bangkok, Tokyo, and Manila permitted it, as the single hold-out against settlement, to exercise extraordinary bargaining power in constantly pressuring for further concessions in Indonesia's favor.[15]

The purpose of this section is to analyze Peking's attempts to encourage Indonesian hostilities against Malaysia and its severance of ties with the West. For Peking, Indonesia's Malaysia policy provided the southern half of a pincer movement in Southeast Asia (the northern being Hanoi) designed to eliminate Western influence from the region. Thus, Peking responded rapidly to Indonesia's official declaration of confrontation in September 1963 with supportive press editorials, which repeated the Indonesian allegation that Malaysia was merely a "scheme" of Britain and the United States to perpetuate neocolonialism. Peking also welcomed the American decision to suspend aid to Indonesia: "The Indonesian people are entirely capable of building their homeland into a prosperous and strong country by relying on their own efforts and on the support of the people of Asia and other parts of the world." [16] The CPR's emphasis on Asian support, rather than bloc support, for Indonesia catered both to Sukarno's own emphasis on regional independence and to Peking's self-perception of China's dominant role over the Soviet Union in regional affairs. In late October, for example, Peking disseminated a Sukarno address calling for an *Asian nationalist* struggle against "necolim" (the Indonesian acronym for neocolonialism–imperialism): "therefore, we should unite the forces of Asia . . . play up Asia . . . and play up the new emerging forces." [17]

[15] For theoretical explanations of Indonesia's bargaining stance, see Fred Iklé, *How Nations Negotiate* (New York: Harper and Row, 1964), p. 58; and Mancur Olson, *The Logic of Collective Action: Public Goods and the Theory of Groups* (Cambridge: Harvard University Press, 1965), p. 41.

[16] *Ta Kung Pao* editorial, September 27, 1963; *People's Daily* editorial, September 29, 1963; and *People's Daily* commentator, September 30, 1963.

[17] NCNA, October 29, 1963.

Peking publicized high-level Indonesian government statements on Malaysia as well as those of the PKI. Two talks by PKI second vice-chairman Njoto in late September and early October were carried by NCNA echoing the Chinese position that the major force behind Malaysia was not really Britain but rather the United States. In an October 6 address, Njoto identified the United States as "the leader of neocolonialism." Thus, the struggle against Malaysia becomes a part of "the revolutionary movement in Vietnam." In a distorted version of Sukarno's NEFO-OLDEFO dichotomy, Njoto declared: "The old established Britain has not been driven out and the new emerging U.S. colonialism has infiltrated deeply into it." As for the U.N. survey of opinion in North Borneo, Peking dismissed it with the following sarcastic remark: "This survey will go down in history as one of the quickest and crookedest public opinion polls ever held. It showed that the United Nations is still functioning on behalf of international monopoly." [18]

The CPR continued its publicity efforts to show the consonance of the PKI with the Indonesian government on national liberation struggles in general and Malaysia in particular. Seizing upon the first anniversary of the Brunei uprising, Peking aired PKI chairman Aidit's ideas on the necessity of continuing Indonesian support for the "Revolutionary Government of the North Kalimantan Unitary State" and the duties of NEFO toward national liberation struggles. Undoubtedly pleased by Sukarno's public association of Indonesian and Chinese security interests in opposing Malaysia, Peking quoted Sukarno's warning that " 'Malaysia' is a neocolonialist scheme aimed at opposing Indonesia and the CPR." [19]

In a major address at a PKI rally on November 12 entitled "The Fight Against Colonialism and Imperialism"

[18] *Ibid.*, October 22, 1963.
[19] NCNA, December 6, 1963.

Aidit outlined the importance of popular uprisings for the realization of Indonesian, and implicitly, Chinese, goals in Southeast Asia.[20] "Evidently popular armed uprising can shake the colonialist power, and since it is capable of shaking it, it is also capable of overthrowing it." As for Indonesia's duty toward such uprisings, Aidit insisted: "As the Socialist countries are duty-bound to render such assistance, the nonsocialist countries such as Indonesia, are also duty-bound to assist the independence struggles waged by other nations and peoples who need assistance. For this reason, we have supported the struggle of the North Kalimantan people at the cost of our lives and blood."

Assured of Chinese support, Aidit concluded by obliquely twitting the U.S.S.R. for its cautious approach to Southeast Asian struggles. After citing the Indonesian people's support for the Soviet Union, Aidit stated: "A socialist country cannot be counted as one if it does not come to the aid of the struggle for independence."

The degree to which the Chinese and PKI lines on revolution coincided is apparent in other Chinese broadcasts of Aidit statements. Aidit was quoted in a talk emphasizing the fact that Southeast Asian revolutions would succeed only with a peasant base. By defeating imperialism in the Asian countries *first,* according to Aidit, "a telling blow will be given to the imperialist forces [which] will be favorable to the revolution in the imperialist countries." [21] In effect, Aidit was signaling to the CCP that the PKI supported its contention that the major "contradiction" between imperialism and socialism lay in Afro-Asian national liberation struggles and not, as the U.S.S.R. held, in Europe-centered economic competition. This position was repeated in a resolution on Southeast Asia passed at the December 23

---

[20] Peking's interest in the Aidit address is indicated by numerous NCNA rebroadcasts between November 26 and December 7, 1963.
[21] NCNA, December 6, 1963.

PKI central committee plenum and disseminated by Peking in late January.[22]

As international pressures from both Western noncommunist and Asian states accumulated for a negotiated settlement to *Konfrontasi,* the PKI urged the government to maintain its initial aim of complete dissolution of the federation. Calculating that the likely forum for negotiation would be Maphilindo, Aidit denounced the prospect "in view of the fact that the domestic and foreign policies of these two foreign countries are not in any way similar to Indonesia's domestic and foreign policies." [23] When, however, negotiations began in January 1964 with Robert Kennedy as mediator, Aidit warned that the PKI would unilaterally obstruct these maneuvers if necessary. In a show of PKI determination and strength, party-controlled rural workers' unions seized British plantations the day after Sukarno's January 18 meeting with the U.S. Attorney General.[24]

Peking, too, appeared taken aback at the Kennedy initiatives and at Sukarno's subsequent talks with leaders of the Philippines, Cambodia, and Malaysia. In hopes of reminding Indonesia not to compromise *Konfrontasi,* but in actuality reflecting Peking's inability to affect any Indonesian decision, a Peking rally was held, devoted to the confrontation theme during the Kennedy-Sukarno talks, in which the United States was depicted as "stepping into the shoes of Britain" in order to use Malaysia "as a base for invading Southeast Asia." An Indonesian diplomat was quoted as saying at the rally that "Malaysia is directed against Indonesia and China. . . . It is our duty to support the people of North Kalimantan *unreservedly.*" [25] (Emphasis added.) On the first day

[22] *Ibid.,* January 27 and 29, 1964.
[23] D. N. Aidit, *Set Afire the "Banteng" Spirit!* (Peking: Foreign Languages Press, 1964), p. 33.
[24] Van der Kroef, "Exporting Indonesia's Revolution," p. 14.
[25] NCNA, January 18, 1964.

of the Sukarno-Kennedy talks, Aidit condemned the "U.S. imperialist threat . . . to impose pressure on the Indonesian people." He appealed: "Our duty is to check the compromising activities of certain persons on the Malaysian issue." [26] (These were the same people, anticommunists in the Cabinet, who would later be tabbed "bureaucratic capitalists" by the PKI.)

With Sukarno's agreement to a cease-fire on January 24 as a prelude to further negotiations, Peking seemed even more upset. Chinese media seized on a Sukarno remark that despite the cease-fire "the goal to eliminate British-created Malaysia will not be changed no matter how tactics may change" and rebroadcast it several times. They also carried an interview with the "foreign minister" of the "Revolutionary Government" of North Kalimantan, who stated that any agreement which might be reached would have "no binding effect on the Revolutionary Government." The Indonesian-sponsored "International Youth Rally of Solidarity with the Liberation Struggle of the North Kalimantan People" also provided propaganda fuel for Chinese furnaces. NCNA dispatches cited several delegates to the Rally, including the Chinese who stressed that "U.S. imperialists . . . will never bestow freedom and independence on the oppressed nations. . . . The people must take up arms to defend themselves." [27] In addition, Aidit was reported to warn Indonesian negotiators: "The Indonesian people . . . do not have the naïve idea that the U.S. imperialists would engage in mediation which would really do no harm to the interest of the Indonesian Republic." [28] Similarly the PKI daily, *Harian Rakjat*, commenting on Kennedy's mission and his supposed accord with Sukarno's principle that Asian problems should be

[26] *Ibid.*
[27] NCNA, January 26, 1964.
[28] *Ibid.*, January 24–25, 1964.

solved by Asians alone, questioned how anybody could believe it "when the U.S. imperialists . . . were trying to
intimidate the entire Asian people by dispatching their
nuclear-equipped fleet to Asian waters. . . . We must guard
ourselves from being deluded by U.S. imperialism. Otherwise, the cause of our people will suffer a severe blow." [29]

In fact, China's fears were unjustified, for under cover of
the Kennedy cease-fire and negotiations in Bangkok in February and early March, Sukarno actually increased the tempo
of his raids in Borneo. With the collapse of the Second
Bangkok talks on March 6, Subandrio claimed that *Konfrontasi* had become an "absolute condition for the further
growth of the Indonesian Revolution." [30] Peking contented
itself with repeating Subandrio's position and citing the
Indonesian Youth Front National Council Statement: "Since
the Second Bangkok tripartite ministerial conference broke
down, the only way out is to carry out more actively the
policy of all-out confrontations against Malaysia." [31]

The Malaysian government also perceived collapse of the
Bangkok talks to indicate a hardening of Indonesia's militance. It responded by introducing mass conscription for
the first time, apparently concluding that only a show of
strength could dissuade Indonesia from pursuing its hostile
policy. Peking reported the Malaysian decision and heartily
endorsed Sukarno's response on March 16 calling for a new
"volunteers campaign," a device which could lead to the
militarization of such strong PKI-led groups as the Indonesian Peasants Association (BTI). Pleased with Sukarno's
renewed threatening position toward Malaysia, Chinese media widely disseminated his statement that "Malaysia threat-
ens not only the security of the Indonesian republic but also

[29] *Ibid.*, January 28, 1964.
[30] Cited in Brackman, *Southeast Asia's Second Front*, p. 219.
[31] NCNA, March 7, 1964.

that of China, Burma, Cambodia, and other countries of Southeast Asia." [32]

Peking's report of Sukarno's August 17, 1964, Independence Day address carried his bitter denunciation of the United States for concluding a limited aid agreement with Tunku Abdul Rahman during his July visit to Washington. The report included Sukarno's warning that Indonesian-American relations were deteriorating in the same way that Cambodian-American relations had deteriorated. The PKI apparently took this as a sign that demonstrations and take-over actions against American interests in Indonesia were now sanctioned and within days launched "popular movements" against the United States. Following his order to encourage Indonesia's pretensions of hegemony in "North Kalimantan," CPR foreign minister Chen I, leader of the Chinese delegation which included Marshal Chu Teh, inferred that Indonesia justifiably had a special defense responsibility in Borneo because its propinquity meant that the two depended "on each other like the lips and teeth," a Chinese expression normally reserved to describe CPR-DRV and CPR-DPRK relations. [33]

When Indonesia, on the anniversary of its independence, shifted from border raids in Borneo to paratroop raids on the peninsula, Malaysia took the dispute for the first time to the United Nations Security Council in September. Indonesia's behavior in the U.N. Security Council once again illustrated Sukarno's peculiar view of international politics. [34] Rather than attempting to deny responsibility for the raids, the Indonesian representative readily admitted

[32] *Ibid.*, March 10, 1964. This statement was indicative of Sukarno's distorted perspective of others' views of Malaysia in that both Cambodia and Burma maintained cordial relations with it during *Konfrontasi*, the former even intermittently providing good offices as a mediator.

[33] NCNA, August 17, 1964.

[34] Only a Soviet veto saved Indonesia from censure.

them, justifying his government's actions by arguing that Indonesia did not recognize Malaysia's existence; therefore, there was no violation of international law! [35]

Peking did not report the Security Council sessions until September 15, perhaps reflecting its own dismay at Indonesia's ingenuousness. Even then it soft-pedaled the delegate's justification of the raids and dwelt instead on his counterallegation of British and American aggression against Indonesia, plus his warning that "an attack by Britain on Indonesia would draw immediate retaliation." Chinese media, however, carefully refrained from linking the CPR specifically with Indonesian military threats against the West. Thus, all reference to Chinese support for possible Indonesian retaliatory attacks against the United States made by Aidit on September 13 were excised from NCNA's report of his speech. Similarly, although the *People's Daily* editorial of September 9 stated that American support of Malaysia was directed against China as well as Indonesia and that "should U.S. imperialism dare to launch aggression against Indonesia, the Chinese people will back the Indonesian people with all their might," subsequent Peking reports of the U.N. Security Council debates and their aftermath stressed Indonesia's ability to defend itself without outside aid. Thus, the September 14 reception and the September 16 banquet given by General Lo Jui-ching for visiting Indonesian Air Force Chief Suryadarma, as reported by NCNA, carried only the routine assurances by the former that "should imperialism . . . launch an attack, it will certainly be utterly defeated by the Indonesian people."

KONFRONTASI'S LAST "TRIUMPH": THE SINGAPORE SECESSION

Between September 1964 and August 1965, Indonesian hostilities followed a predictable pattern of small-scale infiltrations primarily in Borneo and secondarily on the penin-

[35] Cited in Gordon, *Conflict in Southeast Asia*, p. 77.

sula; all raids met with a uniform lack of success, which, of course, was not communicated to the Indonesian public. Peking similarly sustained routine propaganda support. Then, suddenly, *Konfrontasi* received at least a temporary fillip: Singapore's secession from Malaysia in August 1965.

The secession was the result of purely internal Malaysian strains which had been mounting ever since the establishment of the federation.[36] Djakarta, however, saw it differently. Singapore's departure "proved" that Malaysia was an artificial creation and that the "Crush Malaysia" policy was correct. The PKI, fearful lest confrontation be slackened, called for a campaign against both states.[37]

Peking's reaction was more studied. Seeking to diminish the importance of the secession, Chinese media noted that the Malaysian and Singapore governments intended to retain their mutual defense relations. In what may have been the beginning of a bid for a new relationship with Singapore, Peking focused sympathetically on its grievances with Malaya, citing alleged Alliance Party attempts "to foment racial disputes in Singapore" and to interfere "time and again" in matters within Singapore's jurisdiction. Peking also reported Lee's statement of interest in trade with the CPR, U.S.S.R., and Indonesia and his announcement that the Singapore branch of the Bank of China, previously closed by the Malaysian government, would be permitted to function under the new Singapore government. NCNA also

---

[36] A politico-sociological explanation for the separation would include the inability of the two states to form a common political culture and style, leading to mutual mistrust and lack of communication. The slow bureaucratic style of the Alliance in Malaya with its emphasis on private enterprise prosperity through rubber and tin exports antagonized PAP leaders in Singapore who saw their political future to be tied to an industrialized Malaysia and its attendant diversified market. Malaysian requests for more taxes from Singapore were not perceived as a legitimate part of the federal system by the latter, while Lee Kuan-yew's appeal for a Malaysian Malaysia was seen by the Alliance as an attempt to undermine the delicate balance of multi-racial politics.

[37] Brackman, *Southeast Asia's Second Front,* p. 280.

underlined Indonesia's decision to continue confrontation despite Singapore's withdrawal by citing remarks such as Subandrio's that "the question of Sabah and Sarawak could also be solved like that of Singapore, with each becoming a sovereign and independent state." Both Indonesian and Chinese ambivalence over Singapore's independence was indicated, however, in an additional Peking report of a statement by the speaker of the Indonesian Cooperation Parliament which in effect contradicted Subandrio: "We will continue to give support to the revolutionary struggle of the people of Malaya and Singapore and to the struggle of the people of Sarawak and Sabah." [38]

Sukarno, apparently confident that Malaysia's collapse was only a matter of time, revived his special concept of Maphilindo, one which may well have disturbed China in view of its hopes for separate Chinese, Vietnamese, and Indonesian spheres of influence.

> What will be Indonesia's attitude when "Malaysia" has collapsed? We will be willing even to establish a Greater Maphilindo. In this association of truly independent states, such as an independent Indonesia, independent Philippines, an independent Malaya, an independent Singapore, and an independent Sabah, an independent Brunei, and an independent Sarawak, Indonesia will be willing to extend its fullest cooperation and friendship. I have even mentioned the possibility of a Thailand and/or Cambodia joining this thing called Greater Maphilindo. But, of course, all these countries must be truly independent and not manifestations of neo-imperialism or neocolonialism.[39]

Sukarno may well have interpreted Singapore's secession as an opportunity to extend *solely* Indonesian influence in

[38] See NCNA reports of Singapore's secession from August 9 to 17, 1965.
[39] *Indonesian Herald*, August 24, 1965, cited in Brackman, *Southeast Asia's Second Front*, p. 281. Notice that Sukarno made no mention of the Djakarta-Phnom Penh-Hanoi-Peking-Pyongyang axis.

Southeast Asia regardless of ideological proclivities with the CPR. It is noteworthy that the bitterly anti-Chinese, anti-communist, post-Sukarno regime in Indonesia seems to be reviving Sukarno's projection in an anti-communist context. (See the last section of this study.)

Peking's own ambiguity toward Singapore lasted until January 1966, at which time the Chinese seemed to accept the thesis that Singapore's independence was a sham, perhaps because the PAP was engaged in negotiations with both the Soviet Union and the CPR's new enemy, Indonesia. In any case, at a banquet given in Peking on January 12 by the Chinese Committee for Afro-Asian Solidarity, the "Malayan National Liberation League (MNLL) mission" was welcomed. Its head, P. V. Sarma, specifically including Singapore under his aegis, denounced both Malaysia and Singapore as supported by Britain and the United States, and insisted that independence could only be gained by "revolutionary violence . . . the only answer to counterrevolutionary violence." He concluded by condemning "modern revisionists" for establishing contacts with Malaysia—probably an allusion to the November 1965 Soviet-Singapore agreement to establish a trade office and *Tass* post on the island state.[40] As if to reinforce the implications of its reception of the MNLL mission, Chinese media six days later publicized the Havana conference resolutions on "urgent problems," including a statement on Malaya, North Kalimantan, and Singapore. The resolution rejected the latter's "sham independence" branded as "only an intrigue designed by the imperialists to save themselves from total collapse and to establish a rear guard of the Anglo-American imperialists in escalating the U.S. war of aggression in Vietnam to other parts of Indo-China and to China as well." [41]

Thus by 1966, the Sino-Indonesian alliance over the Ma-

[40] NCNA, January 12, 1966.
[41] *Ibid.*, January 18, 1966.

laysian issue—intended to weaken Western influence in the archipelago—had collapsed. The effect of the alliance had actually been counterproductive since while it was in being, British, Australian, and New Zealand forces had been built up in the region. Paradoxically, it took a change of regimes in Indonesia and the disruption of the Sino-Indonesian entente to achieve the diminution of Western influence desired by both Sukarno and Mao. Once Great Britain saw that Indonesia no longer threatened Malaysian independence, economic pressures at home forced London to proceed with troop withdrawals which had been delayed only because of Sino-Indonesian militance in the first place.

4

The Sino-Indonesian Alliance
Part Two: The NEFO Movement

For Sukarno the linkage between the Indonesian and world revolutions was such that there could be no clear-cut boundary between domestic and foreign affairs. As the radical nationalist par excellence on the international scene, Sukarno personified Afro-Asian frustrations with the power distribution in international politics. The slowness of change in power relations combined with the incontrovertible fact that preponderant power lay in the West led Sukarno to the conclusion that the teleology of the system was designed to suppress the Afro-Asian world.

To counter this "given" in the system, Sukarno prescribed the creation of NEFO (the composition of which shifted with changes in Indonesia's friends and enemies; for example, India was included at first but by the mid-1960's was no longer considered a NEFO member because Delhi did not support Indonesian foreign policy). NEFO would "confront" the old power center (OLDEFO) and also build a new world more responsive to the felt needs of the non-Western states. Within this ideological structure, classic nonalignment became irrelevant, a point Sukarno made as early as his address to the 1961 Belgrade Conference. The Afro-Asian states

should no longer content themselves with serving as mediator between the Soviet Union and America but should unite
to wrest control of the system away from the "haves." Sukarno's particular structuring of NEFO, which included the
communist bloc, would have shifted the balance from East-
West to North/West–South/East.

The appropriate setting for NEFO activity, then, would
be Afro-Asian meetings or such variants thereof as the Games
of the New Emerging Forces (GANEFO) and Sukarno's still-
born Conference of the New Emerging Forces (CONEFO).
The purpose of these international gatherings was to solidify
what had theretofore been an unorganized welter of speeches
and state visits into an organizational structure through
which Indonesian leadership would become manifest.
NEFO's heart would be what the Indonesians called the
Djakarta-Phnom Penh-Hanoi-Peking-Pyongyang axis, all of
which were commonly opposed to the U.S. role in world
affairs.

Peking seemed more than willing to reciprocate Sukarno's
NEFO overtures. She permitted Indonesia to use the Chinese-
financed, Afro-Asian front meetings to propagate the NEFO
program, for in effect Indonesian ideology was a virtual
carbon copy of the Chinese Communist proposition that the
task of the oppressed nations is the overthrow of imperialism
and neocolonialism. This consonance reached its apex during
Subandrio's visit to Peking in January 1965. The concluding
joint statement declared that the two states

> share the view that in the present international struggle
> there exist, on the one hand, the imperialist forces, represent-
> ing the old established forces of domination, exploitation, op-
> pression and aggression, and, on the other, the anti-imperialist,
> progressive, and revolutionary forces, being the new emerging
> forces of the world today.

The two parties stressed that no peaceful coexistence is

possible between the new emerging forces and the old established forces or between the imperialist forces and the anti-imperialist forces." [1]

Because the Second Afro-Asian Conference scheduled for July 1965 aborted, there has been only one major NEFO conclave dominated by Djakarta and Peking, GANEFO in November 1963. Indonesia initiated its GANEFO idea seemingly on the spur of the moment after the International Olympic Committee's (IOC) censure in February 1963 of Djakarta's refusal to permit Taiwan and Israel to participate in the 1962 Djakarta Asian Games. When Sukarno withdrew Indonesia from the IOC, he simultaneously called for the creation of GANEFO (probably to regain lost prestige and to "prove" that an Afro-Asian state would not tolerate insult from a Western-dominated international organization): "Pak Bandrio has clearly said that sports cannot be separated from politics. Therefore, let us now work for a sports association on the basis of politics . . . let us create a sports association on the basis of the new emerging forces." [2]

Chinese officials welcomed GANEFO immediately. It presented Peking with a golden opportunity, not only to participate in but also to help organize a new international organization in a field from which the CPR had been previously excluded. It was rumored, for example, that Peking contributed one-half the foreign exchange costs of the Games. Marshal Ho Lung, chairman of the Chinese Sports Commission, declared that China was "willing to play its part in promoting the realization of this proposal." And the Peking press stated that "the peoples in Asia and Africa are fully

[1] Cited in Donald E. Weatherbee, *Ideology in Indonesia: Sukarno's Indonesian Revolution,* Southeast Asia Monograph Series, no. 8 (New Haven: Yale University Press, 1966), pp. 67–68.
[2] Most of the Indonesian material for this discussion of GANEFO comes from Ewa T. Pauker's monograph, *GANEFO I: Sports and Politics in Djakarta* (Santa Monica: The RAND Corporation, July, 1964).

capable of shattering imperialist monopoly and manipulations in international sports." [3]

The PKI expressed equal delight in Sukarno's new sports plan, for it fitted perfectly with the party's own conception of Indonesian foreign policy: "to unify all the new emerging forces of the world," to establish "close cooperation with the Socialist states" and "the anti-imperialist newly independent states." [4] And as the PKI trumpeted at the end of the Games, GANEFO "proves that the East wind is blowing more powerfully than the West wind" and that NEFO holds "absolute superiority over OLDEFO." [5]

Were the hopes of Djakarta and Peking and the enthusiasm of the PKI justified? An examination of the propaganda capital accumulated by GANEFO seems to indicate so.

The Indonesians were gratified because GANEFO proved to be such an attractive international event that some fifty-one countries attended. To be sure, one-third of the countries sent unofficial teams so that those countries which were members of the Olympics would not compromise the status of their best athletes (all GANEFO participants having been threatened by the international sports federations with suspension). The large number of second-rate participants in Djakarta had the practical effect of upgrading the Chinese performance. Peking sent the largest delegation—over 200 athletes—and the most successful. Its athletes won 68 gold, 58 silver, and 45 bronze medals as against the second place country, the USSR, which won 27 gold, 21 silver, and 9 bronze.

China's performance was touted in both Peking and Djakarta media along with widespread coverage of Sukarno's many speeches which played the anti-imperialist, anti-colo-

[3] *Peking Review,* 8 (February 22, 1963): 8–9; *People's Daily,* February 13, 1963.
[4] D. N. Aidit, *Set Afire the "Banteng" Spirit!, Ever Forward, No Retreat* (Peking: Foreign Languages Press, 1964), pp. 33–34.
[5] *Ibid.,* p. 5.

nialist themes to the hilt. Indeed, during the course of the Games, the GANEFO slogan, "Onward, No Retreat!" was manipulated by Sukarno so that it also became the new anti-Malaysia battle cry.[6] Despite Indonesia's use of the Games for militant foreign policy ends, however, Indonesian hospitality also served to refurbish somewhat her general image as a member of the international community, which had been damaged during 1962–63 by Djakarta's repeated hostile statements and aggressive actions.

A close examination of Peking's treatment of the Games yields some insight into both its developing entente with the Sukarno regime and its early hopes for the NEFO movement. In order to create the spirit of joint planning and organization before the Games occurred, Chinese officials invited an Indonesian delegation to witness elimination matches on the mainland and to meet the Chinese athletes who would journey to Djakarta.

Ten days prior to the November 10 opening of the Games, Peking was already saturating the Asian air waves with details of the aims of GANEFO and the enhanced camaraderie it would generate among the Afro-Asian–Latin American participants. The major themes of this propaganda buildup were made manifest in late September: (1) that GANEFO was designed to counteract the U.S.-dominated IOC; (2) that GANEFO was a progressive step along the road of Afro-Asian–Latin American solidarity emanating from the spirit of Bandung—thus associating it with a more pacific period in both Chinese and Indonesian foreign policy; and (3) that the CPR was associating itself with the common struggle of all new emerging nations to develop their own national sports policies on an independent basis, that is, to wean them away from Western-controlled international sports organizations.[7]

Buttressing Indonesia's already adamant opposition to the

<hr />

[6] Pauker, *GANEFO I*, p. 16.
[7] See for example, the *People's Daily* editorial, September 23, 1963.

IOC, while depicting the Olympic Committee's censure of Indonesia as an official U.S. policy, Peking declared:

> U.S. imperialism and its hirelings have attempted to obstruct the convocation of the Games. They insist on Indonesia's recantation of its just stand in sponsoring the Fourth Asian Games last year as the condition for its participation in the 1964 Olympic Games in Tokyo. They also made the Executive Council Meeting of the IOC adopt an arbitrary "resolution" calling on the Olympic Committees of all countries not to participate in GANEFO. This is a notorious insult to the dignity of Indonesia and all countries in Asia, Africa, and Latin America which uphold the Bandung spirit and support GANEFO.
>
> The Chinese people look upon the Games as an excellent opportunity to promote their friendship with the people of Indonesia and other new emerging countries . . . they also hold that the Games are useful in strengthening the Asian, African, and Latin American peoples' fight against imperialism and colonialism and in defense of world peace.[8]

As for the IOC charge that Indonesia was combining sports and politics during the Asian Games, Professor Ma Yeuh-han, "dean of Chinese sports officials," replied:

> I know from my own experience that the development of sports in a country is closely connected with its political, economic, and cultural development. . . . Finally contacts between sportsmen of China and other countries have increased particularly since the Bandung Conference. . . . This is favorable to the people in the various Asian, African, and Latin American countries and unfavorable to imperialism.[9]

Indonesian officials went even further in their hopes for the Games when Sports Minister Malidi announced that GANEFO is aimed at "breaking up the old system and build-

[8] *Ibid.*, June 27, 1963.
[9] NCNA, June 29, 1963.

ing a new one in international sports." [10] And on November 6, even before the Games began, Peking quoted the Indonesian delegation leader Colonel Jonosewajo's announcement that "the first GANEFO would lay the foundation for future games of the emerging forces." [11]

During the course of the Games, Chinese media provided reportorial coverage and editorial comment through the Peking press and NCNA. The thrust of this treatment was strongly anti-American, depicting the United States as GANEFO's major opponent.

Typical were charges that U.S. officials were manipulating the IOC

> as an instrument for their encroachment upon the sovereignty of other countries and their discrimination against the new emerging countries. IOC chairman, U.S. imperialist element Brundage, openly clamored that those who want to participate in the GANEFO would be subject to dismissal by the IOC. Behold, how clamorous and unreasonable is this U.S. imperialist element who wormed his way into the rank and file of international sports.
>
> It goes without saying that the GANEFO is an embodiment of the Bandung spirit and a manifestation of the irresistible historical current in the international arena. . . . Now the GANEFO has broken the imperialist monopoly of international sports and will usher in an era of vigorous growth and progress in this field. . . . However fervently the imperialists and reactionaries may pray for the failure of the GANEFO, it will shine even brighter like the morning sun.[12]

Despite the euphoric terms with which Peking described GANEFO and its vilification of the Olympics, an examination of the propaganda output indicates that the latter was still perceived to be the standard against which GANEFO's

---

[10] *Ibid.*, September 20 and October 30, 1963.
[11] *Ibid.*, November 6, 1963.
[12] *People's Daily* editorial, November 10, 1963.

success should be judged. Numerous comparisons, for example, were made between the sportsmanship displayed at GANEFO versus that at the Olympics, as well as the respective attendance records. Claiming new international sports records set at the Games, one Chinese paper remarked: "Every good record created at the Games as well as the new sportsmanship displayed will be a resounding slap in the face for the imperialists . . . and colonialists who are sparing no efforts to belittle the significance of the meet after having failed to prevent its opening.[13] Finally citing the PKI's *Harian Rakjat*, NCNA quoted: "The imperialists might not recognize these records, but their recognition was not needed. These records . . . have been established as an iron-clad fact, and they cannot be erased." [14]

As the Games drew to a close, the Chinese achieved several propaganda payoffs. First of all, the bonds between Indonesia and the CPR seemed more firmly tied than ever before. In exchange for Indonesia's providing access to yet another Afro-Asian forum, the Chinese responded by broadcasting the mass rallies in Djakarta which linked GANEFO with Indonesia's confrontation policy against Malaysia. These rallies were designed to convey the impression both in Indonesia and abroad that *Konfrontasi* had acquired Afro-Asian support. Secondly, Peking used the Games to promote PKI fortunes within Indonesia. During Vice-Premier Ho Lung's public meeting with PKI leaders, the leaders' appeals for a NASAKOM cabinet (one composed of nationalist, religious, and communist elements) were reiterated in the context of support for GANEFO and confrontation. Finally, GANEFO became yet another forum for Chinese efforts to convince the Afro-Asian–Latin American states to reorient their inter-

[13] *Ibid.;* and the Chinese sports newspaper, *Physical Culture,* November 12, 1963. Interestingly, even the opening ceremony at GANEFO emulated the Olympic torchbearer.

[14] NCNA, November 14, 1963.

national outlook away from the West (and perhaps implicitly the U.S.S.R.).

Although Peking did not explicitly identify the Soviet Union as one of the states opposed to GANEFO (the Soviets sent an athletic contingent most of whom were not of Olympic caliber), Pyongyang did. Having its own difficulties with the U.S.S.R. at this time, North Korea may have objected to the lukewarm Soviet attitude toward the Games:

> The Korean people and youth will do everything in their power for the victory of the Games of the New Emerging Forces and will firmly unite with the peoples of Asian, African, and Latin American countries in the struggle for smashing the machinations of the imperialists and the *modern revisionists* against GANEFO. [Emphasis added.] [15]

In an editorial marking the conclusion of the Games, Peking expressed its hope for their institutionalization:

> GANEFO is proof that the people of the New Emerging Forces are quite capable of developing their sports and other work independently and successfully. . . . [It is] the urgent demand of the people of new emerging countries and the world to insure that GANEFO opens every four years. . . . It is obvious that any action contravening this demand will seriously damage the fundamental interests of the people of the new emerging countries in the field of sports and games. [16]

Chinese propaganda, summarizing the effects of the Games on their participants, developed the notion of a community of interest between the CPR and the developing countries which would extend from the sports realm to other issue-areas. The Games themselves were depicted as the quintessence of sportsmanship and fair play in contrast to the alleged ubiquitous racial discrimination of the Olympics. [17] Related

---

[15] Pyongang Domestic Service, November 10, 1963.
[16] *People's Daily* editorial, November 23, 1963.
[17] See, for example, *Ta Kung Pao*, November 23, 1963.

to the discrimination theme was the Chinese argument that smaller states could compete more readily in GANEFO because its rules were more flexible than those of the Olympics: "in other international competition we have often witnessed the big nations bullying the smaller ones; but this has never happened at GANEFO." [18]

The CPR's first significant breakthrough on the Games came, not surprisingly, from Cambodia, which decided to rescind its offer to host the Olympic-affiliated Southeast Asian Peninsular Games and apply the experience gained from the first GANEFO to a similar contest in Cambodia in 1964. Thus, at least one country moved in the direction Peking and Djakarta were pushing.

Peking was careful to publicize Indonesia's sponsorship of the Games, while underplaying its own role and confining self-praise to the publication of Indonesian remarks on the excellence of Chinese athletics. Thus, the head of the Chinese delegation at GANEFO's close attributed its success "to the care of President Sukarno . . . ," and NCNA cited Indonesian experience in the "protracted struggle against imperialism and colonialism," observing that "Indonesia's excellent organizing at GANEFO has won the admiration of sportsmen from all parts of the world." Ho Lung, on the conclusion of his stay, hailed success of the Games as "a manifestation of the outstanding organizational capability of the organizer of the GANEFO, the government and people of Indonesia . . . another event of tremendous historic importance following the Bandung Conference." [19]

The CPR was undoubtedly pleased with the results of the GANEFO Congress (held immediately after the conclusion of the Games), in which Peking became one of the three vice-chairmen of GANEFO representing Asia. In addition to

[18] NCNA, November 18, 1963.
[19] *Ibid.*, November 19 and 22, 1963.

institutionalizing the Games, the Congress provided China
with an opportunity "to endorse the basic principle against
imperialism and colonialism"—GANEFO's political basis—
in the preamble to the Congress documents.[20]

Moscow appeared both embarrassed and annoyed at GAN-
EFO's success, despite the fact that the U.S.S.R. became its
European vice-chairman. The Soviets feared GANEFO's
negative impact on their Olympics position and, more important, the opportunity it gave China to project the polemic
into a new international forum. To put the best appearance
on Moscow's unhappy position, *Tass* stated:

> The nature of the activities of Soviet representatives in the
> international Olympic movement is determined by the spirit of
> internationalism, the sense of great responsibility to the pro-
> gressive forces of the world, to the young states of Asia, Africa,
> and Latin America. Realizing the necessity of strengthening the
> unity of the world sports movement, the Soviet youth support
> the idea of the GANEFO, which, as conceived, do not stand in
> opposition to the Olympic Games.[21]

THE ASIAN BLOC AND NEFO

Sukarno's rapprochement with China was followed by
friendly overtures toward the other members of the Asian
bloc, North Korea and North Vietnam, with whom diplomatic relations were established in April and August 1964,
respectively—less than a year after GANEFO. Sukarno
seemed to be particularly impressed with Kim Il-Song's
industrialization program for the DPRK, with its emphasis
on self-reliance, which, after Sukarno's visit, became embodied in the new Indonesian slogan, *berdikari* ("self-reliance"). Sukarno cited North Korean achievements frequently

[20] *Ibid.*, November 24 and 25, 1963.
[21] *Tass*, November 25, 1963.

after his November 1964 trip to that country and urged Indonesians to emulate them in solving agricultural production problems.[22]

Pyongyang seemed quite willing to cater to Sukarno's egomania by liberally employing such appellations as "steadfast antiimperialist" and "national hero of Indonesia" during his stay as well as by awarding him an honorary degree from the DPRK Academy of Science. Kim declared that Indonesian-Korean "solidarity [had] developed to a new stage. The peoples of our two countries are comrades-in-arms fighting against imperialism and colonialism." [23]

Sukarno, on his part, viewed North Korea as an additional ally for both domestic and foreign affairs. In an address to a Pyongyang rally, he stated: "The Korean and Indonesian people should assist each other in the great revolutions we are now undertaking. . . . Only when the closest international cooperation exists between us can we bring the international imperialist forces to their knees, smash and overthrow them." [24] And in an earlier banquet speech, he noted: "Korea is building socialism . . . with great success. Well, we in Indonesia are also working hard to establish . . . a socialist society." [25]

The joint communiqué's quid pro quo consisted of Indonesian support for Pyongyang's stand on Korean unification in exchange for the latter's "undivided support and militant solidarity" for Indonesian confrontation. More significantly, the communiqué contained the first official expression of outside support for Sukarno's pet project, a conference of the new emerging forces (CONEFO) which would include "all independent countries in Asia, Africa, and Latin America, the socialist countries, and all progressive forces in other

[22] Weatherbee, *Ideology in Indonesia,* pp. 43–44.
[23] Korean Central News Agency (KCNA), November 4, 1964.
[24] KCNA, November 2, 1964.
[25] *Ibid.,* November 1, 1964.

parts of the world." [26] On a one-day stopover in Shanghai, where Chou En-lai unprecedentedly flew to meet him, the Chinese Premier praised Sukarno for "holding aloft the banner of anti-imperialism and anti-colonialism" at the recently concluded second nonaligned conference in Cairo and claimed that because of Sukarno's steadfastness "very favorable conditions for the second Afro-Asian conference" had been created. Sukarno replied that Indonesia and China were "close friends . . . and comrades-in-arms, fighting shoulder to shoulder in the same struggle." [27] Earlier in his August 17, 1964, Independence Day address, at which time Peking had also urged early convocation of a second Afro-Asian conference, Sukarno had indirectly expressed some qualms that the Sino-Soviet dispute could embarrass Indonesian efforts to facilitate Soviet participation in the conference which had been initiated after Mikoyan's June 1964 visit to Djakarta and Moscow's attendant promise of more military aid. In August, Sukarno hoped that "the issue of who will participate in the forthcoming Afro-Asian conference will not cause disunity . . . because such would harm the solidarity of the anti-colonialist and anti-imperialist forces." [28] After his November visits to North Korea and China, it is noteworthy that no similar plea emanated from Djakarta. It is conceivable that the promises of North Korean support for CONEFO and complete Chinese backing in the Second Afro-Asian Conference led Sukarno to soft-pedal diplomatic initiatives on behalf of the U.S.S.R.

Sukarno also mended fences with North Vietnam, taking the occasion of the August 1964 independence celebration to announce the establishment of full diplomatic relations with Hanoi at the embassy level, characterized by the latter as a "splendid manifestation . . . of close solidarity [and a]

[26] *Ibid.*, November 4, 1964.
[27] NCNA, November 5, 1964.
[28] Djakarta Domestic Service, August 17, 1964.

new stage in the friendly relations between our two countries." [29] Foreign Minister Subandrio praised the "iron solidarity" between the DRV and Indonesia because "the fate of
the two nations is identical . . . threatened and encircled
by the imperialists." [30]

In reporting Sukarno's address, Peking highlighted his
identification of the history and aspirations of Indonesia with
those of Cambodia, the DPRK, and DRV, referring to the
southern halves of the latter two states as their "West Irians."
Quoting Sukarno, the Peking report stated: "No evil spirit,
no genie, no devil can prevent Korea, Vietnam, Cambodia,
and Indonesia from . . . uniting themselves in the march
toward a new world." [31] PKI Chairman Aidit went even further in portraying Sukarno's speech as actually leading to
a "Djakarta-Phnom Penh-Hanoi-Peking-Pyongyang defense
front." [32]

The propaganda/diplomatic effects of the DRV's new rela-
tion with Indonesia were manifested during the latter's wran-
gle in the U.N. Security Council in September over Indonesia's direct infiltration into Malaya. A North Vietnamese
Foreign Ministry note iterating Indonesian countercharges,
condemned British and American "aggression" against Indonesia while the Hanoi press declared that "the so-called
Malaysia is the second frontline of the imperialists [after
Indochina] to oppose the independence . . . of Southeast
Asian countries." [33]

Diplomatic activity among Indonesia's new "axis" partners
accelerated in late 1964 and early 1965. In late November
and early December, Chinese Foreign Minister Chen I visited
Djakarta without prior announcement and conferred with
both government and PKI leaders. The joint press release

[29] Vietnam News Agency (VNA), August 17, 1964.
[30] Djakarta Domestic Service, August 25, 1964.
[31] NCNA, August 18, 1964.
[32] *Ibid.*, August 19, 1964.
[33] VNA; and *Nan Dhan* editorial, September 13, 1964.

concluding Chen's visit seemed to carry Sukarno's November Shanghai statement even further. At that time, the Indonesian President had declared "the Chinese and Indonesian governments are standing and fighting on the same battlefront . . . against all imperialists and neo-colonialists." The December 3 joint press release called for a linking-up of all "anti-imperialist struggles" into a single common front in which "all the new emerging forces in the world must support each other." Apparently anticipating strategy for the then upcoming Afro-Asian conference, the joint press release urged that unity against imperialism everywhere in the world should be one of the main tasks of the conference.[34] By unity, it is obvious that both parties meant an endorsement of Peking's conception of national liberation movements and perhaps even the extension of material aid from sympathetic countries to these movements. (The "freedom fighters" of North Kalimantan would, of course, be among the deserving recipients.) As the Indonesian Information Ministry concluded: "The danger posed by the joint action of the imperialist countries is not to be dealt with separately, but should be opposed with a common struggle of the Asian-African countries." Such a policy of lumping together all Sino-Indonesian opponents (presumably including such states as India and Malaysia) and encouraging revolution against them did not augur well for Soviet plans to use Indonesia as its entrée into the Afro-Asian forum. The U.S.S.R., at least since its 1960 failure of direct intervention in the Congo, had eschewed blanket support of leftist violence, focusing instead on political cooperation with incumbent nationalist parties which were prepared to maintain independence from the West.

Attesting to the complete consonance of Indonesian positions with those of the Asian bloc since August 1964 was Kim Il-Song's April 1965 state visit to Indonesia. Expressions of

[34] NCNA; and Indonesian Information Service, December 3, 1964.

mutual admiration and "comradeship-in-arms" punctuated his stay. North Korea's self-reliance was touted by both Kim and Indonesian leaders. Significantly, the concluding communiqué manifested Indonesian endorsement for a number of Asian bloc positions couched in Sukarno's NEFO language:[35]

the new emerging forces of the world can liquidate imperialism only by uniting and fighting in a single, united front;

the forthcoming Afro-Asian conference must be the cornerstone for an antiimperialist united front of all the new emerging forces;

U.S. actions in Vietnam are "strongly condemned," and the two leaders agree that "the only way" to solve the Vietnam situation "lies in the discontinuation of the U.S. aggression in Vietnam and the unconditional withdrawal of U.S. troops and bases from South Vietnam;

denunciation of the United Nations as a "pliable tool of the imperialists" [Indonesia's withdrawal is discussed below];

mutual endorsement of Indonesia's confrontation and North Korea's unification goal.

During the visit of Kim, as well as that of Chou En-lai who arrived for the tenth anniversary of the Bandung Conference, Sukarno pressed vigorously for a 1966 CONEFO. Kim readily repeated his endorsement of November 1964, but Peking was silent. Carrying Sukarno's plan further, Deputy Premier Charul Saleh stated that the Second Afro-Asian Conference would be "paving the way toward the holding of CONEFO," which would establish "a more representative

---

[35] Djakarta Domestic Service, April 15, 1965.

and powerful world organization to replace the obsolete United Nations." [36]

At first, however, Peking chose to ignore Sukarno's CONEFO campaign.[37] Sukarno, nonetheless, attempted unilaterally to associate the CPR with his position. In a rally speech he declared: "the CPR is giving assistance in the construction [of the CONEFO building] because CONEFO is in the interest of the CPR as well as other nations within the NEFO group." [38] Whatever the cause of Peking's hesitance to endorse CONEFO, Chou did at least mention it in a favorable context prior to his departure from Indonesia. At a farewell reception, he acknowledged Indonesian efforts on behalf of the Afro-Asian conference, noting almost in passing that Sukarno was also "preparing for the holding of CONEFO." [39] Peking's reticence might be explained by the Chinese calculation that it did not want to dilute the Second Afro-Asian Conference's potential impact by devoting attention to still another future conference; there may also have been some annoyance that Indonesia had planned CONEFO on its own, without permitting the Chinese to inject their views and goals. In any case, Chou's statement could hardly be termed a ringing endorsement. The PKI, on the other hand, displayed much more enthusiasm for CONEFO. Aidit strongly endorsed it in Sukarno's own terms at the PKI central committee plenum in May. The Second Afro-Asian Conference and CONEFO would establish "offensive diplomacy in the international arena . . . in order to create a

[36] *Ibid.*, April 18, 1965.

[37] NCNA, April 20, 1965, for example, in reporting Sukarno's cornerstone ceremony for the CONEFO building, changed its title to the "international political venues building," dropping any mention of CONEFO.

[38] Djakarta Domestic Service, April 19, 1965.

[39] NCNA, April 26, 1965. Such Chinese reticence would also fit Guy Pauker's speculation that some Sino-Indonesian differences were developing prior to the Algiers Conference over Soviet and Malaysian participation, each partner fearing the other would sell out. Guy Pauker, "The Rise and Fall of Afro-Asian Solidarity," *Asian Survey*, vol. 5, no. 9 (September, 1965).

most intensive revolutionary atmosphere in Africa, Asia, and the world." [40]

INDONESIA'S U.N. WITHDRAWAL:
A NEW STAGE IN SINO-INDONESIAN RELATIONS

Sukarno's growing disenchantment with the United Nations, despite its assistance in Indonesia's annexation of West Irian, was readily acknowledged by students of world politics. The Michelmore mission's conclusion supporting the creation of Malaysia and the barely disguised censure of Indonesia in September 1964 by the Security Council—avoided only by a Soviet veto—should have indicated to Sukarno the gap between his vision of the future of the Afro-Asian world and the hopes of most leaders from these states. The Afro-Asian and Latin American votes against his assault on Malaysia in September were a setback for Sukarno. Bolivia, Morocco, and the Ivory Coast submerged any ideological affinity for Indonesia in a larger interest—the strengthening of the U.N.'s moral position as a protective shield for smaller powers. Given his "outlaw" policies, Sukarno may well have calculated that continued U.N. membership would only prove a constant source of embarrassment. Malaysia's election to the Security Council provided a convenient excuse for Sukarno dramatically to declare his country's withdrawal on the last day of 1964. Again, though he may have hoped that Indonesia's exist would initiate a trend among the Afro-Asian states, he was sorely disappointed. In light of Indonesia's manifest isolation, it becomes particularly noteworthy that Sukarno's subsequent CONEFO campaign and his stress on an Asian radical "axis" would serve to integrate Indonesia into an international subsystem more to Sukarno's ideological temperament. At the same time, Indonesia's U.N. withdrawal could pave the way for its refusal to give the

[40] D. N. Aidit, "Political Report to the Fourth PKI Central Committee Plenum," May 11, 1965, in JPRS (Joint Publications Research Service), *Translations on South and East Asia*, 91 (August 9, 1965): 55.

international organization jurisdiction to implement the West Irian agreement and also set the stage for the day when Indonesia might withdraw from the partial nuclear test-ban treaty.[41] Echoing Peking, Sukarno declared that Indonesia would rejoin the United Nations only when it was "retooled" to provide greater recognition to NEFO.[42] After Indonesia's withdrawal, it became increasingly apparent that Sukarno had opted to link Indonesia with the Asian bloc in order to revise the old Asian power distribution.

Although the CPR may not have been privy to the making of Sukarno's decision, it rapidly capitalized on its impact. Within a week, the Peking press was publishing paeans of editorial praise, setting the tone for a January 10 government statement which remonstrated: "more and more facts have shown that the United Nations has been increasingly reduced to a tool of imperialism and old and new colonialism headed by the United States." As for Afro-Asian confidence in the world organization, the Peking press lamented: "The increase in the number of Asian and African members in the United Nations has by no means brought about any fundamental change in the fact that the United Nations has become a U.S. imperialist instrument for aggression." [43]

China's total disaffection from the United Nations had come about in a little over a year. As recently as December 1963, Peking had declared: "The Chinese Government has, however, always judged the activities of the United Nations on their intrinsic merits. We resolutely oppose all evil doings of the United Nations, but will have no objection to the good things, if any, done by the United Nations." [44] With

[41] Brackman, *Southeast Asia's Second Front,* p. 241.
[42] Cited in Alastair M. Taylor, "Sukarno—First United Nations Dropout," *International Journal,* 20, no. 2 (Spring, 1965): 308. The degree of Afro-Asian opposition to Indonesia's withdrawal was displayed by a joint appeal by the UAR, Yugoslavia, and Ceylon (conveners of the Cairo Conference) asking that Sukarno reconsider.
[43] *People's Daily* editorial, January 10, 1965.
[44] *Ibid.,* December 21, 1963.

Indonesia's withdrawal, however, Peking perceived new opportunities to substitute an Afro-Asian forum for the world body and thus avoid the fact that, even if admitted to the United Nations, the CPR would be constantly on the defensive against both the Soviet Union and the United States.

Thus, Peking's portrayal of the United Nations in January 1965 debunked "blind faith" in it and insisted that China's exclusion "has not harmed us a whit." The press praised "the experiences of Indonesia, Cambodia, and Cuba" which show that "it is precisely by resisting U.N. intervention that these countries have asserted their own sovereignty and safeguarded their own security."

The necessity of "remolding" the United Nations threads through Chinese propaganda on Indonesia's withdrawal from the January 10 government statement through the republication of statements by Afro-Asian leftists. On January 21, NCNA even carried PNI chairman Hardi's call for the "establishment of a new United Nations—of the new emerging forces." Demonstrating that the CPR may well have been favorably reassessing Sukarno's CONEFO idea, Chou En-lai in mid-January announced that the CPR would entertain the possibility of establishing a rival, "revolutionary" United Nations. Later in his account of an interview with Mao in February, Edgar Snow reported that the Chinese leader foresaw a new United Nations as a natural progression from such gatherings as the Afro-Asian Confeernce and GANEFO, "a potential permanent assembly of the have-not nations, to exist independently from the American-dominated United Nations." [45]

Cognizant that Indonesia would require more than propaganda support if China hoped to replace Soviet influence

---

[45] Cited in Byron S. Weng, "Communist China's Changing Attitudes Toward the United Nations," *International Organization*, 20, no. 4 (Autumn, 1966): 699.

completely, Liu Shao-chi proclaimed that "the Chinese government and people, if they can make some contribution to Indonesia's self-reliance, will consider it a boundless honor." [46] Peking also publicized Indonesian press assurances that the country could count on assistance from the Asian bloc and on appeals by Indonesian officials of the Indonesian-Chinese Friendship Society for unity "with our Chinese comrades-in-arms . . . with Djakarta, Phnom Penh, Hanoi, Peking, and Pyongyang as its axis." [47] No doubt the specifics of such aid were discussed during Subandrio's late January visit to Peking in which he was accompanied by an entourage that included military men. It is possible that an unannounced arms agreement was reached at this time, which may even have included a promise of nuclear assistance.[48]

The Indonesian foreign minister's trek to Peking served to carry forward the theme of a common Afro-Asian struggle against imperialism—implicitly led by the CPR and Indonesia—previously enunciated during Chen I's visit to Djakarta in November 1964. Now, Maoist and Sukarno world views were juxtaposed in a joint statement—describing the world's antagonistic forces: "on the one hand, the imperialist forces, representing the old established forces of domination . . . , and, on the other, the anti-imperialist . . . forces, being the new emerging forces of the world today. . . . No peaceful coexistence is possible between them."

Appraising Subandrio's visit, Chen I termed it significantly "a new stage" in Sino-Indonesian relations, perhaps because for the first time at the Indonesian foreign ministry level, Subandrio had affirmed: "we have a common enemy—imperialism headed by the United States and Britain!" [49] None-

[46] Peking Domestic Service, January 12, 1965.
[47] See, for example, NCNA reports of January 14 and 20, 1965.
[48] After Subandrio's Peking visit, Sukarno referred increasingly to the prospect of Indonesian nuclear testing.
[49] NCNA text of Subandrio address, January 28, 1965.

theless, the specifics of Chinese support for Indonesia, at least publicly, remained equivocal. Both Chou En-lai's banquet address welcoming Subandrio on January 24 and the concluding joint statement merely asserted: "Should the British and U.S. imperialists dare to impose a war on the Indonesian people, the Chinese people will absolutely not sit idly by." Chou had prefaced his pledge by deprecating "motley" British and American military strength in Southeast Asia.[50] Subandrio's farewell address also hinted that the Chinese may have disappointed Indonesia's military aid hopes. Referring to "mutual assistance" needs to expel America and Britain from the region, not only did he omit specific mention of Chinese aid but added: "They described to us both good and rather bad experiences which enlightened us somewhat." The Peking press also emphasized Indonesia's *independent* capability to confront Malaysia.[51] While Peking reported no specifics of military aid to Indonesia, Djakarta media claimed that the CPR had given a new fifty million dollar credit in addition to a similar amount pledged by Chen I the previous November.[52]

Subandrio and Chen I in their joint communiqué agreed that the United Nations "must correct its mistakes and be thoroughly reorganized," but they stopped short of repeating Chou's warning that a rival "revolutionary" organization "may well be set up." [53] An Indonesian interview with Chou sheds some light on the ambiguity of the Chinese position: on the one hand, derogation of a body in which the United States and the Soviet Union exercised predominant influence, and, on the other, a desire not to oppose the Afro-Asian states which insisted on staying with that body. Although quoted as repeating his appeal "to consider the organization

[50] *People's Daily* editorial, January 30, 1965.
[51] See the *Ta Kung Pao* editorial, January 29, 1965.
[52] Djakarta Domestic Service, January 30, 1965.
[53] Nonetheless, the January 30 *People's Daily* editorial endorsed Chou's proposal.

of a revolutionary United Nations outside the existing United Nations," Chou conceded that "some African and Asian countries believe that it is better to carry out the struggle in the United Nations by making corrections. Let us invite them to do so. . . . We are not going to obstruct them." [54]

Finally, it is worth noting that the development of Peking's stance on the United Nations between 1965 and 1967 illustrates the rapidity with which the Sino-Soviet polemic had accelerated. Whereas in January 1965 Chinese officials and media employed only such generic terms as "revisionists" in condemning those who practiced coexistence in the United Nations, by 1967, after the U.N. Security Council debates on the short-lived Arab-Israeli war, the authoritative Peking press fulminated:

> The United Nations has done all sorts of evil things and is incapable of doing anything good precisely because it has become a place where the big powers make dirty deals with one another and an instrument of the United States and the Soviet Union for pushing ahead with their "power politics." . . . The so-called United Nations is, to put it plainly, nothing but an organization for the United States and the Soviet Union to decide on the fate of other countries. [55]

Seeing an opportunity to revive his earlier proposal, which had lain dormant for some months, for a rival United Nations at a banquet for envoys from the Arab and African states, Chou once again demanded that the U.N. "must correct all its mistakes of the past [and] be thoroughly reorganized and transformed" to achieve "the equality of all countries, big and small," or else "the possibility that a new revolutionary United Nations will be set up will increase." [56] Nonetheless, Chou again conceded that "friendly Afro-Asian

---

[54] ANTARA, January 27, 1965.
[55] *People's Daily* Commentator, June 28, 1967.
[56] NCNA, June 24, 1967.

countries can wage struggles inside the United Nations," implicitly acknowledging once more that China's leverage in the politics of international organizations was extremely limited and that its perception of the aspirations of the "third world" was disorted by ideological myopia.

5

CPR-Indonesian Linkage: The PKI

Up to this point we have discussed the consonant external goals of the Chinese and Indonesian governments as a major component in the development of a Sino-Indonesian entente. We shall now examine another major linkage between the two states: the existence within Indonesia of a political organization committed to changing the Indonesian political system into a socialist state, if not under the direction of, certainly in harmony with, the world view of the Chinese Communist Party (CCP). Thus, Peking possessed two sources of influence on Indonesian policy-makers: (1) such common state goals as the destruction of the Western position in Southeast Asia and (2) the operations of the PKI designed to foster internal changes within the regime. Schematically, this influence flow appears as set forth in the figure on page 8 above.

The importance attached by the CCP to the PKI may be understood by the simple fact that the combined membership totals of the two parties accounted for about one-half of the world total of all communist parties' members. As the 1960's unfolded, CCP-PKI cooperation increased, although the latter insisted on maintaining complete autonomy over

its own operations in both domestic and international communist affairs.

There were essentially two avenues available to the CCP
for influencing the Indonesian government through the PKI.
The avenue most appealing to Peking would probably have
been for the PKI to serve as its satellite or fiduciary, simply
carrying out instructions determined by China. Such a relationship, however, would parodoxically have weakened the
PKI's ability to serve Chinese ends, for it would have destroyed the PKI's credibility as an *autonomous* Indonesian
political party. The other avenue along which Chinese influence could be exerted was through the demonstration of
common, though independently determined, goals and a subsequent coordination of strategies for Indonesian development. During the 1960's it was this latter avenue on which
the PKI and CCP seemed to be successfully traveling up to
the time of the coup. To achieve an effective working relationship with the PKI, however, the CCP had to tolerate
"revisionist" practices they were unwilling to accept in other
parties.

In terms of CCP dogma the PKI's cooperation with noncommunist Indonesian leadership in Sukarno's cabinet and
his rubber-stamp parliament was unconscionable. As early as
1959 and again at the 1960 Moscow Conference, Mao had
insisted that an indigenous communist party in a revolutionary situation must provide its own, sole source of leadership and not be content merely with membership in a coalition of equals. Such dogma led the CCP to reject the Moscow
Conference's formulation of an "independent national democratic state." This concept provided ideological justification
for communist support of noncommunist governments in
the underdeveloped world which were willing to break ties
with the West and establish new bonds with the socialist
states. To the Chinese, such a formulation would ultimately
lead to a sellout of local communist revolutionary opportuni-

ties.[1] But, in fact, the PKI seemed to be following precisely this strategy from the late 1950's and Sukarno's enunciation of "Guided Democracy." As early as February 1957, the PKI had picked up and backed Sukarno's notion of a NASAKOM cabinet (a cabinet composed of nationalist, religious, and communist elements—according to Sukarno, the three pillars of the Indonesian revolution).[2]

Such early PKI support for Sukarno did not mean there was no intra-party conflict over party policy or even that the CCP did not try to intervene. Indeed, there is indirect evidence suggesting considerable discontent among the more impatient, radical elements within the PKI, perhaps with CCP support, to whom the Aidit leadership continually was forced to justify its policy. Thus, in September 1963, Aidit argued defensively at a Peking rally: "The demand for the formation of a NASAKOM cabinet at present is therefore an important part of the struggle to achieve our strategic objective. Here the Indonesian Communists consider the question of forming a NASAKOM cabinet as one affecting the balance of force. In the last analysis, it is a question of revolution, and not one of 'structural reform.' " [3] Just two months later, party theoretician Njoto defended PKI adherence to Sukarno's 1959 Political Manifesto in similar terms against allegations by "dogmatists" that the party was permitting Sukarno to determine the direction of the Indonesian revolution:

In MANIPOL it is explicitly stated that our revolution has two stages; that the present stage, the first, is an antifeudal, anti-imperialist, national-democratic revolution; and that the later stage, the second, is socialist revolution. Although no

[1] For a discussion of Chinese objections to the Moscow Conference's impact on strategy in the Third World, see Richard Lowenthal, " 'National Democracy' and the Post-Colonial Revolution," in Kurt London, ed., New Nations in a Divided World (New York: Frederick A. Praeger, 1963).
[2] See the article on the history of the PKI in Red Flag, May 20, 1963.
[3] D. N. Aidit, Some Questions Concerning the Indonesian Revolution and the Communist Party of Indonesia, Report at Peking Rally, September 4, 1963 (Peking: Foreign Languages Press, 1964), p. 87.

statement is made regarding the leadership of the proletariat
in the revolution, since the working class and the peasant class
are recognized as being pillars of the revolution then it is
impossible for the socialism that is collectively aspired to by
the Indonesian people to be bourgeois socialism or false socialism.[4]

As he put it in Peking, "Embodied in the Political Manifesto
and the Economic Declaration, progressive political and economic plans for carrying out the Indonesian revolution have,
in effect, become official policy." [5]

In a formulation much closer to the Soviet notion of the
"national democratic state" than to the Chinese concept of
party-led permanent revolution, Aidit rationalized the PKI's
close cooperation with Sukarno by claiming that the Indonesian "bourgeois democratic revolution . . . is one of a new
type and a part of the world proletariat socialist revolution
firmly opposed to imperialism." In apparent deference to
Chinese objections, however, as well as to the PKI's own
goals for Indonesian development, Aidit concluded: "It is
the historic task of the proletariat to contend for its leadership." [6] It is noteworthy that Aidit made no effort to clarify
how the party would go about assuming the leadership of
the Indonesian revolution. Rather he seemed to place the
party's future in Sukarno's own "progressive" proclivities
and the normal evolution of events within the country.

Aidit stressed the consonance between Sukarno's MANI-
POL and the PKI's own two-stage revolution, labeling NASA-
KOM as the link between the two and the party's opening
wedge to a position of power. Although, Aidit acknowl-

[4] *Harian Rakjat,* November 3, 1963, in JPRS, *Translations on South and
East Asia,* 47 (December 31, 1963): 8.
[5] Quoted in *Peking Review,* 37 (September 13, 1963): 38.
[6] D. N. Aidit, *The Indonesian Revolution and the Immediate Tasks of the
Communist Party of Indonesia,* Report Developed at Higher Party School of
the CCP Central Committee, September 2, 1963 (Peking: Foreign Languages
Press, 1964), pp. 14–16.

edged, "the present day state power in the Republic of Indonesia, like any other state power, is also a machine in the hands of the ruling class to suppress other classes," nonetheless, this power includes a "progressive aspect" under Sukarno, which has become the "main aspect." [7] Such PKI demands as the "retooling of bureaucratic capitalists" (to be discussed below) were designed to strengthen the progressive forces at the expense of the reactionary and hence facilitate the transformation of the Indonesian Revolution into one under more direct PKI control. Such a development would meet the CCP's objection that the public sector of a bourgeois state was really controlled by capitalists unless seized by representatives of the proletariat.[8]

Aidit seemed to have good reason to interpret the secular trend of Indonesian affairs as being in the PKI's favor. As he put it in February 1963: "Despite the fact that we have sometimes been 'tripped up' or 'had our feet hobbled' by the state apparatus itself, we have nevertheless, within a period of only two years, succeeded in building up an organization of the National Front throughout. . . . This is a very great accomplishment, and it is due to national Gotong Royong [cooperation] with NASAKOM as the fulcrum under the leadership of Bung Karno." [9] Furthermore, Aidit was led to believe, the Indonesian president was prepared over time to tap the PKI for national leadership and thus fulfill the CCP dictum of a party-led revolution: "Bung Karno writes about the need for a genuine *vanguard party*." (Emphasis added.)[10] Given the developments of the 1960's, he assumed Sukarno meant the PKI, for the Indonesian president's vague notions of "Guided Democracy" and "Guided Economy" dovetailed with the PKI's theory of the two-stage revolution. The en-

[7] *Ibid.*, pp. 34–37, 42.
[8] See *Red Flag*, October 1, 1959.
[9] D. N. Aidit, *Dare, Dare, and Dare Again!* (Peking: Foreign Languages Press, 1963), pp. 9–10.
[10] *Ibid.*

gendering of a frenetic nationalist atmosphere was already leading to the destruction of liberal organization in Indonesia and toward active collaboration with the communist world.

As inferred in the opening chapters of this study, much of the PKI's domestic success could be attributed to Indonesia's increasingly radical external policies. For example, the significance of *Konfrontasi* for the PKI lay in the fact that the party had been the first Indonesian political group to oppose the creation of Malaysia when it was proposed in 1961. By 1963 the PKI's earlier lone position had become the new orthodoxy. Under cover of MANIPOL, according to one observer, the Malaysia campaign represented a significant PKI breakthrough into the inner circle of Indonesian foreign policy decision-making.[11]

Sukarno's radical nationalist foreign policy, first displayed in West Irian and then in *Konfrontasi,* provided the PKI with the ammunition it needed to respond to domestic and perhaps foreign critics of its policy of cooperation with Sukarno. In his report to the Central Committee in December 1963, Aidit, citing Indonesia's action in West Irian and Borneo, asserted: "In Indonesia, it is not only the people but also the Government that is waging a struggle against imperialism." [12] That the CCP was neither unaware nor opposed to the PKI's successful strategy was evident from *Red Flag*'s May 1963 issue which hailed the party's domestic and foreign lines: "Its influence and prestige in international affairs is increasing day by day."

In part the CCP's enthusiasm for the PKI despite its "unorthodox" domestic tactics reflected Peking's pleasure at the growing pro-Chinese attitude of the Indonesian party, which

[11] Justus M. Van der Kroef, "Indonesian Communism's Cultural Offensive," *Australian Outlook,* 18 (1964): 40–61; and his "Indonesian Communism and the Changing Balance of Power," *Pacific Affairs,* 37, no. 4 (Winter, 1964–65): 359.
[12] D. N. Aidit, *Set Afire the "Banteng" Spirit!, Ever Forward, No Retreat!* (Peking: Foreign Languages Press, 1964), p. 97.

began with muted criticism of the U.S.S.R.'s de-Stalinization program in 1961 and became quite vocal by 1963. Nonetheless, the PKI itself insisted that whatever position it took in the international communist movement resulted from autonomous deliberation rather than orders from an outside authority. As early as December 1961, in a central committee resolution, the PKI went even further than the polycentrism of the Italian communist Togliatti in arguing: "We do not agree with the theory of many centers, because . . . we do not agree with the existence of a central system in the world communist movement." [13] Significantly, where the CCP criticized Togliatti for his "revisionist" formulation, no such objection was raised to the PKI resolution. Peking undoubtedly viewed the PKI as a valuable linkage group to the Indonesian polity, one that should be cultivated for its influence-potential on Sukarno rather than reprimanded for scholastic deviation from Maoist dogma. During this period the Chinese still possessed tactical flexibility.

Beginning in 1963, Chinese media increasingly publicized PKI pronouncements which supported the CCP in the polemic, including PKI denunciation of Yugoslavia; its support for China on the Sino-Indian border war; and, upon his return from visits to both the Soviet Union and China in September 1963, Aidit's insistence that Southeast Asia had become the focal point of "the most acute anti-imperialist struggle" in the world, a struggle which must be led by indigenous Marxist-Leninist parties.[14] Reviewing the revolutionary potential of the region, Aidit emphasized the importance of peasant-based actions and insisted that by defeating imperialism in the Asian countries *first*, "a telling blow will be given to the imperialist forces [which] will be favorable to the revolution in the imperialist countries." [15]

---

[13] *Harian Rakjat,* January 2, 1962.
[14] Justus M. Van der Kroef, "Indonesian Communism's Changing Balance of Power," pp. 373–75.
[15] Reported by NCNA, December 6, 1963.

He took exception to the Soviet view "that continued armed
struggle against colonialism and imperialism is no longer
important or significant" by arguing that some "excolonial
states" will not shift the world balance of power, because,
like Malaysia, they are still committed to the West. Even
Indonesia's foreign policy, Aidit charged, is free "in name
only, since these policies are still checked by the imperialist
groups that still have economic power in Indonesia. . . . Indonesia is still a part of the oppressed nations of the world,
and therefore she must still continue to struggle against
colonialism and imperialism." [16]

While reprinting statements by both sides in the polemic,
Harian Rakjat tended to carry the Chinese statements in
full, while printing abridged versions of those of the Soviets.
In August 1963, the PKI took the Chinese side by condemning the partial nuclear test-ban treaty as it "legalizes the
'big three'" and called on the NEFO nations to develop
their own nuclear weapons. Peking rewarded these PKI
gestures by providing a red-carpet treatment for Aidit in
Peking the next month and by making him an honorary
Academica Sinica member.

In his December Politburo report—the PKI's first public
exposé and analysis of differences with the CPSU conducted
under the transparent proxies of the "Dange clique," "Yugo-
slav revisionists," and "some comrades"—Aidit challenged
the "status quo" attitude of "some people" who believe that
communism could be built in one country while imperialism
was still oppressing others. He criticized the Soviet tactical
shift to economic competition as aiding indiscriminately
all countries regardless of their progressive or reactionary
qualities under the false assumption that newly independent
states would automatically follow the socialist path. Echoing
the Chinese position, Aidit asserted that, contrary to Soviet

[16] *Harian Rakjat,* November 14, 1963, in JPRS, *Translations on South and
East Asia,* 48 (December 31, 1963).

ant Society (BTI) had to convince the peasantry that their interests could not be served by traditional religious and secular authorities.[23] By 1963, for example, in his plenum report, Aidit claimed that the party had section committees in eighty-three per cent of the villages.

When the 1960 Agrarian Law on crop-sharing was passed and ran into insurmountable landlord obstruction, the PKI chose to pass itself off as the legitimate representative of the peasant, unexceptionably working within Guided Democracy to achieve the tiller's legal rights. In fact, the party was hoping to shift peasant allegiance away from traditional village heads toward the party. If successful in this enterprise, the party could perhaps convince Sukarno that it was the best organization for him to utilize in achieving other national goals.[24] As Aidit saw it as far back as 1956, the PKI's blueprint for the assumption of power (peaceful or otherwise) should be "to change the balance of power between the imperialists, landlords, and other *comprador* bourgeoisie on the one hand, and the people on the other, by arousing, mobilizing, and organizing the masses." [25] To achieve this end, the PKI's agrarian goals were reformist, not revolutionary. The party promoted more equitable product allocation and land distribution rather than class revolution in the countryside, despite its militancy with respect to national liberation movements in general.

The PKI's emphasis on constructing a mass party rather than an elitist party for competition in the Indonesian polity

[23] See Donald Hindley, "Political Power and the October 1965 Coup in Indonesia," *Journal of Asian Studies* (February, 1967); and Daniel S. Lev, "Political Culture in Indonesia: Some Comments" (Paper presented at the Meeting of the Association for Asian Studies, Chicago, March, 1967), pp. 17–18.

[24] See Ruth McVey's "Indonesian Communism and the Transition to Guided Democracy," in A. D. Barnett, *Communist Strategies in Asia* (New York: Frederick A. Praeger, 1963), pp. 178–88.

[25] Quoted by Guy T. Pauker, "Indonesia: The PKI's Road to Power," in Robert Scalapino, *The Communist Revolution in Asia: Tactics, Goals and Achievements* (Englewood Cliffs, N.J.: Prentice-Hall, 1965), p. 262.

with its attendant problems of communication and command structure may well have contributed to the party's rapid disintegration in the aftermath of the coup. This will be discussed later. Perhaps the party leadership calculated that it need not remain conspiratorial so long as Sukarno was increasing its status and prestige. In any case, by mid-1964 it was apparent that the requisites of building a mass following had taken precedence over the maintenance of a tightly-knit party organization. As Sudisman put it, of the twenty-two "duties" of party members and committees, fully ten of these consisted of promoting new party memberships, despite his acknowledgment that the party's size had created factional and discipline problems.[26]

By 1964, the party evidently felt it had enough backing from Sukarno to initiate demands for the "NASAKOMization" of land reform committees and land reform courts to remove landlord elements from positions of obstruction and to replace them with party-controlled representatives of the BTI. Aidit warned that if the implementation of the Agrarian Law was further delayed, the PKI would back "the emergence and spread of unilateral actions by the peasants." [27]

The BTI initiated unilateral land seizures in mid-1964 through the forced occupation of private and *public* lands, the seizure of harvests, and the destruction of forest reserves. The party may well have underestimated the resistance it would meet, for head-on clashes occurred with the military in the guise of regional governments, with Moslem groups representing landholders, and even the PKI's sometime ally, the PNI, which controlled competing peasant organizations. In response to this opposition, at its July First National Conference, a party resolution demanded the NASAKOMization

[26] *Harian Rakjat,* July 9, 1964, in JPRS, *Translations on South and East Asia,* 59 (August 7, 1964): 11–15.
[27] Aidit, *Set Afire the "Banteng" Spirit!,* pp. 24–27; and Aidit's call for such actions at the forty-fourth PKI Anniversary in *Harian Rakjat,* May 16, 1964.

of regional governments which allegedly were controlled by members of the outlawed Darul-Islam and the Indonesian Socialist Party. In a little over a year, confident of the party's strength in the villages, Aidit proposed the direct election of village heads to be followed by the NASAKOMization of the state apparatus.[28]

Peking endorsed the PKI's pressure on the peasant front, particularly after Sukarno himself seemed to support it. For example, Aidit's research on the peasant movement in Java, conducted in February 1964 and probably a conscious replication of Mao's effort in Hunan in the 1920's, was published in a special *Red Flag* supplement in January 1965. In concluding his assessment Aidit declared, probably with some accuracy: "The class division of the villages shows that the working people in the countryside are barbarously exploited and oppressed by the following: (1) despotic landlords, (2) usurers, (3) seedling buyers, (4) bureaucratic capitalists, (5) dishonest brokers, (6) bandits, (7) corrupt local officials."

During June and July NCNA carried numerous reports of BTI-sponsored, unilateral land seizures and the PKI First National Conference resolution on the NASAKOMization of Land Reform Courts and land reform committees. But NCNA had also reported the PKI's willingness to bargain with local officials, that is, to call off its land seizures in exchange for effective enforcement of the Agrarian Law and crop-sharing agreements: "If the landlords no longer carry out 'unilateral actions' on their part, indiscriminately harming the peasants . . . and those unscrupulous officials who maladminister these two laws are punished, naturally, the unilateral actions taken by peasants . . . for the consistent implementation of the law on crop-sharing agreements and the basic agrarian law will no longer be necessary." [29] Thus,

[28] D. N. Aidit, *Political Report to the Fourth Central Committee,* May 11, 1965, in JPRS, *Translations,* 91 (August 9, 1965): 25, 32.
[29] *Harian Rakjat,* June 29, 1964.

by 1965, both Peking and the PKI viewed the party's prospects favorably despite increased rural opposition. The party and Sukarno seemed to be moving in tandem.

THE PKI AND THE POLEMIC

The PKI's very insistence on party autonomy in the 1960's tended to place it more on the Chinese than on the Soviet side of the polemic, for it was the former which had challenged Soviet supremacy at the 1960 Moscow Conference and carried the burden for the small party. The PKI opposed the U.S.S.R.'s decision to expel Albania "because in this way we did not join in creating a bad precedent of Communist and Workers' parties attacking each other at the congress of a party." [30] Aidit feared that dissension among parties would lead to the development of factionalism *within* parties as well. The PKI opposed readmission of Yugoslavia into the socialist community because of its willingness to deal with the West and for disseminating the idea of a "third road" for underdeveloped states. Significantly, PKI opposition to Yugoslavia dovetailed with both the Chinese and Sukarno's own projections for the Afro-Asian world. Aidit described the Afro-Asian world much the way Lin Piao would a full twenty-one months later as "the village of the world, while Europe and North America are the town of the world." [31] But most of all, the Indonesian party, like the CCP, was exercised by Moscow's decision to discuss Stalin's misrule—a prospect which could only explode other parties' pretensions to infallibility and utopia.

As early as the December 1961 central committee plenum, the PKI insisted that there was no longer any center of international communism. By the December 1963 plenum, Aidit implied that the PKI was moving even further away from the CPSU when he inferred that both revisionism and

---

[30] Aidit, *Dare, Dare, and Dare Again!*, p. 61.
[31] Aidit, *Set Afire the "Banteng" Spirit!*, p. 87.

dogmatism could be applied to the same party, obviously the CPSU: "It is very likely indeed that the modern revisionists are at one and the same time modern dogmatists because both have one and the same starting point, that is subjectivism." [32]

There was another reason for Aidit's displeasure over the mutual recriminations of the polemic, namely, the difficulties created for internal PKI goals because of them: "Our experience in Indonesia shows that when serious differences arise in the international communist movement and are not correctly dealt with, they can become a great obstacle to the consolidation of the national united front, because our allies in the antiimperialist struggle will not feel secure to rely on the Communist Party." [33]

Indicative of the PKI's opposition to Soviet pressure on other communist parties to dampen the flames of revolution was Aidit's statement after his 1963 journey to both the U.S.S.R. and CPR, that Marxist-Leninists, when faced with revisionism, "have the complete right to propagandize their views outside the Party, and to form circles and associations and put out a magazine, and even establish a new party." Pinpointing the party to which he was referring, Aidit called on "true Marxist-Leninists" to take over the leadership of the Indian Communist Party (CPI) from the "Dange clique" and assured them that "the PKI will maintain contact with the new communist party in a country if that particular party is effectively established as a corrective counter-force against the old party and the revisionists. . . ." [34]

Aidit's main concern seemed to be that the Soviet formulation would supersede the independent role of indigenous communist parties for the advance to socialism, allowing

[32] *Ibid.*, p. 68.
[33] D. N. Aidit, *The Indonesian Revolution and the Immediate Tasks of the PKI*, p. 46.
[34] *Harian Rakjat*, October 4, 1963, in JPRS, *Translations on South and East Asia*, 43 (November 19, 1963): 34–35.

them only a subordinate role as "servants of the bourgoisie, like the Dange Clique in the CPI." [35]

The NCNA summary of Aidit's plenum speech of December 23, 1963, disseminated his appeal for the formation of rival Marxist-Leninist parties in those countries where the incumbent parties "are under the control of revisionists." This entreaty fitted the Chinese injunction presented by Chou Yang in his October 26 speech to CCP intellectuals, an address that was not released by NCNA until two months later, however. That the PKI was as good as its word was revealed in Calcutta in January 1965 during interrogations of arrested members of the pro-Peking CPI who disclosed that finances for their activities had come through PKI channels.[36]

NCNA also publicized the PKI December 1963 plenum resolution on revisionism which included Aidit's classification of communist parties into four groups.[37]

(1) Marxist-Leninist parties including the PKI;
(2) parties whose leadership is controlled by the revisionists but in which there is Marxist-Leninist opposition;
(3) parties under the complete control of the revisionists, but where expelled Marxist-Leninists have set up Marxist-Leninist organizations; and
(4) parties whose leadership is under the complete control of the revisionists, but where new communist parties have been set up side by side with them.

According to the Chinese, this anti-revisionism resolution linked the PKI struggles against revisionism and imperialism.

The PKI extended its fight against revisionism not only to the CPI but also to the then pro-Peking majority group

[35] Aidit, *Set Afire the "Banteng" Spirit!*, p. 94.
[36] Justus M. Van der Kroef, "Indonesian Communism's Expansionist Role in Southeast Asia," *International Journal*, 20, no. 2 (Spring, 1965): 203.
[37] First published in *Harian Rakjat*, October 4 and 5, 1963.

within the Japan Communist Party (JCP). In September 1964, JCP Secretary General Miyamoto visited Djakarta to obtain PKI support in his bitter dispute with the CPSU, less than two weeks after the JCP's letter to the Soviets denouncing them for "grossly interfering in JCP affairs." Chinese media broadcast the PKI/JCP joint statement which attacked "modern revisionism" for purveying the "utter falseness" that the United States under Kennedy and Johnson had acquired "common sense" and was "peace loving." It charged that the imperialists were capitalizing on the difficulties created by the modern revisionists to weaken the socialist camp. Because of this, the PKI expressed its "full support" for the JCP decisions to expel the "revisionist clique of Shiga and Suzuki" (JCP members expelled from the party in May after voting for the partial nuclear test-ban treaty in the Japanese Diet and accused by the JCP of having maintained surreptitious contacts with the CPSU in order to split the JCP and create a new party).[38]

The bitterness of this attack was so pronounced that Moscow for the first time openly responded to the PKI, criticizing the joint statement for making "bitter attacks" on those "who have been untiringly fighting for peace and friendship among nations." The joint statement, Moscow media charged, echoed the "hatred toward mankind preached by the Peking splitters." Insinuating that the PKI had fallen out of step with Sukarno, Moscow reminded the PKI that the Indonesian Government had both signed the test-ban treaty and expressed gratitude for Soviet aid in the liberation of West Irian.[39]

The PKI's virtually total split from the CPSU was manifested when Aidit refused the Soviet invitation to the com-

[38] NCNA, September 11, 1964. For a fuller discussion of the split in the JCP, see Sheldon W. Simon, "New Soviet Approaches to the Japanese Left," *Asian Survey*, vol. 5, no. 6 (June, 1966).
[39] Radio Moscow in Indonesian, September 17 and 18, 1964.

munist parties' meeting in Moscow scheduled for March 1, 1965. Chinese media disseminated Aidit's justification for refusing to attend because the meeting "was merely intended officially to declare a split in the international communist movement." Imitating the Chinese, Aidit charged that "modern revisionism without Khrushchev still exists, and this is proved by holding the schismatic meeting in March 1965." [40]

Solidifying its bond with the CCP at the forty-fifth PKI anniversary celebrations in May, Aidit stated in the presence of both Chinese and Soviet delegations: "The PKI and the CCP are as close as flesh and blood in the struggle against the twin brothers—imperialism and modern revisionism. . . . We hold that the CCP is a red beacon-light in upholding Marxism-Leninism and combatting modern revisionism." [41] Just three days earlier, Aidit elevated "modern revisionism" to the status of one of "the five devils" along with Malaysia, the United States, bureaucratic capitalists, and the "seven village evils."

Finally, just two months before the abortive coup, Aidit spent over two weeks with CPSU leaders in Moscow and Bucharest, presumably in an unsuccessful effort to paper over their differences. That this gambit did not succeed was indicated by the lack of any joint communiqué issued upon his departure.

Sukarno Moves toward PKI Hegemony: First Stage

As has been postulated in this study, the CPR possessed two susceptible influence groups in Indonesia: the PKI and the group around the president. When Sukarno began to act as though the PKI were his prime domestic supporter in 1964, the Chinese may well have concluded that Indonesian politics had shifted from a center position between the U.S.S.R. and CPR toward the Chinese pole.

[40] NCNA, May 24, 1965.
[41] NCNA, May 26, 1965.

As the Army-instituted State of Emergency was lifted in 1964, the military lost much of its ability to control PKI activities through martial law. Aidit felt sure that from Sukarno's 1962 "Year of Triumph" Independence address, the president would gradually move the country toward PKI control. As Aidit saw it, NASAKOM, *Pantjasila*, and MANIPOL—the three main Sukarno shibboleths—were "part of one unit which cannot be separated in the efforts of the Indonesian people to finish the national-democratic revolution and proceed toward Socialism." [42] In other words, Aidit cast Sukarno in the role of the national-democratic leader who, with PKI assistance, would conduct Indonesia through the anti-feudal stage of the revolution. As we shall see below, Sukarno's 1964 Independence Day address added new weight to this interpretation.

A number of developments unfolded during the course of 1964 which exhilarated both Peking and the PKI. The government's own indoctrination courses, incorporating a Marxist-Leninist outlook, came increasingly to resemble the PKI's cadre courses. By decree, Sukarno abolished the Army-controlled Committee for Retooling the State Apparatus (PARAN) and replaced it with KOTRAR, on which the PKI was represented.[43] In the provinces the party agitated to eliminate anti-communist officials, concentrating on the anti-communist governors of Atjeh and West Java. Simultaneously, Aidit was conducting a survey of Javanese tenant conditions, the results of which were designed to assist any prospective PKI government to plan agrarian policy. Unilateral peasant actions, also led by the PKI, were likewise designed to exert pressure on the government to provide a new avenue for PKI representation (through its peasant affiliate) on the newly proposed land reform courts. Sukarno

[42] Cited in Pauker, "Indonesia: The PKI's 'Road to Power,'" p. 281.
[43] Donald E. Weatherbee, *Ideology in Indonesia: Sukarno's Indonesian Revolution* (New Haven: Yale University Press, 1966), p. 47.

seemed to bend to this pressure when he agreed in September to the establishment of the courts and the creation of a cabinet committee on agrarian affairs to which the PKI leader Njoto was appointed. The party had high hopes for the land reform courts because they fell under the jurisdiction of the Minister of Justice, Astrawinata, a crypto-communist who could be counted on assuring appropriate BTI representation. Increased party control of rural Indonesia would, *over time,* help to solidify its peasant base for any ultimate showdown the party might face with the military, which was aligning itself increasingly with Moslem landowners in the face of a commonly perceived PKI threat.[44]

In what was to prove a prophetic insight into the dynamics of rural Javanese fanaticism which was often led by Moslem landlords, Aidit warned: "The results of the research in West Java, which subsequently were strengthened by the results of research in East Java and Central Java, clearly prove that the landlords hold the economy of the villages in their grip and that they have a great influence in village life." [45]

Nonetheless, despite the PKI's realization that the party was far from being home free, Aidit was obviously very pleased with the trend of events up to and including Sukarno's 1964 Independence Day speech. As he put it in an address to the Peking Higher Party School in September: "In Indonesia's present political situation, the enemies of communism are unable openly to launch political attacks on the PKI, since many of the Party's political viewpoints have already been incorporated in state documents." [46]

It was Sukarno's Independence Day address which gave the PKI a virtual green light. In the course of his speech, Sukarno clearly linked Indonesia's future with that of the Asian

[44] *Harian Rakjat,* July 9, 1964, in JPRS, *Translations on South and East Asia,* 59 (August 7, 1964): 5.
[45] *Harian Rakjat,* August 1, 1964, in *ibid.,* 61 (September 10, 1964): 29.
[46] Aidit, *Immediate Tasks of the PKI,* p. 32.

bloc: "The Indonesian revolution aims at socialism. . . . If there is a science I follow, this is because I know the message of the people's suffering, because I know speculation, because I know a most important science, namely Marxism." [47]

Chinese media picked up Sukarno's endorsement of the PKI position on land reform courts and unilateral land seizures as well as his agreement with the PKI that political parties should not be consolidated, a suggestion raised earlier by the national-Marxist Murba party in hopes of diluting PKI strength.[48] Chinese media also repeated the PKI Politburo statement praising Sukarno's decisions on these two issues and an Indonesian national front statement demanding the prosecution of "all violators of the basic agrarian law . . . in accordance with the president's independence address." [49]

Urging the PKI on to further actions against foreign-owned enterprises in Indonesia, Sukarno fulminated: "Let me stress that basically and ultimately no imperialist capital must be allowed to operate on Indonesian soil." And finally, placing himself squarely behind the PKI appeal for participation at all levels of Indonesian political life, Sukarno insisted: "Whoever is against NASAKOM is not progressive. Whoever is against NASAKOM is in fact crippling the revolution. . . . Whoever is against NASAKOM is . . . in fact a historic conterrevolutionary." [50]

Small wonder that Aidit saw Sukarno as the national leader who would not only permit the PKI to ride his coattails but also determine his direction. As an earnest of Sukarno's good faith, Aidit pointed out to party skeptics that both he and Lukman had attained ministerial rank in 1962 when Sukarno inflated his cabinet by conferring such status

[47] Djakarta Domestic Service, August 17, 1964.
[48] NCNA, August 17, 1964.
[49] NCNA, August 18 and 24, 1964.
[50] Djakarta Domestic Service, August 17, 1964.

on speakers of parliament and vice-chairmen of the Provisional People's Consultative Congress.

When, directly following TAVIP's strong pro-PKI endorsements, Sukarno appointed PKI Second Deputy Chairman Njoto and crypto-communist Oie Tjoe Tat of *Baperki* as ministers attached to the cabinet presidium, Aidit seemed to conclude that the time was ripe for a new campaign to promote the creation of a NASAKOM cabinet. In his September address at the Peking Higher Party School, he explained the PKI's vision of Indonesia's two-stage revolution and NASAKOM's place within it: "The demand for the formation of a cabinet of Mutual Help and Cooperation with NASAKOM as its core is a tactical demand to realize the future strategic demand: the people's government or the people's democratic government." [51]

Indeed, the PKI had been able by 1963 to mobilize extra-party support for NASAKOM from other leftiest Indonesian parties, including the PNI, Partindo, Perti, and some leaders of NU and PSII. In the succeeding two years, the party also managed to infiltrate and organize parts of the intellectual community where it had traditionally been quite weak. In an August 1965 speech to the Second Congress of People's Writers and Artists, organized in 1964 (the year of TAVIP), Aidit underlined Sukarno's support of such Congress objectives as the creation of "communist artists and writers . . . [who] are not liberal but want to be and can be led by the party." He urged revolutionary artists to move to the villages "in order to exterminate the remnants of feudal culture in the village [for] the essence of our revolution is an agrarian revolution or a peasants' revolution. . . ." [52] And in a contemporary greeting to the Indonesian Scholars Association,

---

[51] Cited in Van der Kroef, "Indonesian Communism's Changing Balance of Power," p. 368.
[52] *Harian Rakjat,* August 28, 1965, in JPRS, *Translations on South and East Asia,* 97 (October 6, 1965): 13–17.

Aidit expressed his pleasure at policies leading to the introduction of Marxism-Leninism at the university level: "Now the principle of 'knowledge for the people and revolution' may be said to have won over the principle, 'knowledge for knowledge's sake'. . . . Now more and more demands are made that Marxism be taught in all universities by competent persons, i.e., Marxists taken from the PKI ranks."[53]

Sukarno's TAVIP endorsement of the PKI was not greeted with unadulterated joy by all elements of Indonesian political life. Both the military and liberal intellectual groups organized in hopes of blocking the communist juggernaut. The attempts, however, were half-hearted and indirect, no group being willing at this time to challenge the PKI on the political grounds of subversion so long as the party possessed the Bung's blessing. The first attempt by liberal intellectuals to insulate themselves from the deadening hand of Marxist-Leninist control was embodied by the Cultural Manifesto of 1964 (MAINEKIBU). PKI pressure led to its being banned in May, whereupon several groups including Murba and the army organized the Body for Promoting Sukarnoism (BPS), the purpose of which was to challenge the PKI's interpretation of Sukarno's dicta. However, since Sukarno was the ultimate judge of his own teachings, which he chose to link with the PKI, the BPS was also shot down by presidential decree on January 6, 1965. In effect, Sukarno and the PKI had declared that opposition to the radicalization of Indonesian life was illegitimate and proof of counter-revolutionary tendencies.[54]

Nevertheless, the BPS did give the PKI some bad moments by raising issues which the PKI under freer political conditions probably could not satisfactorily have answered, issues which would be remembered by the Indonesian populace

[53] *Harian Rakjat,* August 25, 1965, in *ibid.,* pp. 29–30.
[54] Weatherbee, *Ideology in Indonesia,* pp. 51–52.

after the abortive coup. For example, the BPS press charged the PKI with plotting a coup, introducing as evidence for the allegation what appeared to be authentic documentation of future PKI strategies. Although Aidit hotly denied the charge in December at Bogor, he did not choose to refute the evidence.[55]

Aidit had committed a tactical blunder in October by implying that once socialism was achieved in Indonesia, there would no longer be a need for *Pantjasila*. The BPS press seized upon this statement as proof that the PKI was a "false *Pantjasilaist*." Moslem outcry against the PKI was silenced only by Sukarno's intervention and was repressed until the bloody aftermath of the Coup, when the earlier BPS press charges were seemingly vindicated.

It is certainly conceivable that the PKI appealed for external support and pressure from Peking on the BPS issue. At least one observer feels that it was CCP pressure on Sukarno which was instrumental in his decision to ban the BPS in December 1964 and Murba the following month.[56] In any case, Peking was quick to publicize both developments, branding the BPS an organization which "had in fact given rise to a split in the ranks of the revolutionary and progressive national forces." [57] On the same day Peking media carried Sukarno's January 6 decision to ban Murba "temporarily." It also disseminated Aidit's condemnation of Murba as a group of "bureaucratic capitalists" (a likely reference to Deputy Minister Charul Saleh who was associated with Murba and had been a long-standing PKI target) who "even dream of setting up a communist party, which would surely be a revisionist one." [58]

[55] Aidit, *Report to Fourth Plenum*, May 11, 1965.
[56] Harold C. Hinton, *Communist China in World Politics* (Boston: Houghton Mifflin, 1966), p. 414.
[57] NCNA, December 18, 1964.
[58] NCNA, January 7, 1965.

THE CHINESE, SUKARNO, AND THE
PKI FORTY-FIFTH ANNIVERSARY

The PKI's forecast of a two-stage Indonesian revolution and Sukarno's own promotion of NASAKOM were meshing beautifully. As Aidit put it at the party's forty-fifth anniversary celebration on May 23, 1965, the President had agreed that the PKI was the staunchest defender of the Indonesian revolution, that its policies adhered to the dual anti-feudal and anti-imperialist lines of Sukarno's program, and that resistance to PKI agrarian reform actions would not be tolerated. When such resistance was sustained, despite Sukarno's admonition, by right-wing PNI elements in Java, Sukarno ordered the party in August 1965 to purge itself of "false *Marhaenists*," a move which virtually completed the destruction of the PKI's organized domestic political enemies less than one year after the banning of the BPS and Murba.[59]

Sukarno's exhortation: "Go ahead, PKI!" became the signal for renewed PKI pressures to lower prices and obtain land reform after the May 1965 party anniversary, a program conducted through such mass organizations as Gerwani, SOBSI and the BTI. At one point Sukarno's enthusiasm for the PKI and Indonesian socialism threatened to take the initiative away from the party. In an address on April 11, the Bung declared that Indonesia was about to enter the "socialist stage," in which land reform would be completed and foreign capital eliminated. The party was faced with the delicate question of refuting Sukarno on this point without insulting him. In a theoretical piece on the stages of the Indonesian revolution, the PKI insisted that the transition to socialism would occur in Indonesia only when all feudal elements in the society were destroyed and when

---

[59] Arthur J. Dommen, "The Attempted Coup in Indonesia," *China Quarterly*, (January–March, 1966): 160–64.

the party had assumed the transitional leading role.[60] Reasoning defensively that the PKI accepted its own special interpretation of *Pantjasila* which provided legitimacy but did not subordinate it to any other Indonesian power center, a May 1965 Politburo statement stressed: "The attitude of the PKI in accepting the *'Pantjasila'* is scientific and objective and does not mean at all that it has become a revisionist party." [61]

Beginning with the May anniversary, the party directed its ire at the alleged "alliance" between the PKI's domestic enemies—"Trotskyites" and "bureaucratic capitalists"—and the imperialists. Praising Indonesia's success in destroying the American position in the country since 1963, the party press proclaimed:

> At the first plenary session about two years ago, it was merely stated that U.S. imperialism was enemy number one; the second plenary session discussed the steps to be taken against U.S. imperialism; and only after the third plenum was underway was the boycott against American films carried out which was led by the central boycott action committee. But now all American imperialist capital has been taken over. This is truly a very valuable victory . . . achieved mainly thanks to the growing strength of national unity with NASAKOM as its core.[62]

In his political report on the anniversary, Aidit expressed gratitude and pleasure at Sukarno's destruction of the PKI's enemies and then turned his guns on the last bastion of anti-PKI strength, the army which, in the guise of bureaucratic capitalists, Aidit admonished, was still able to "collaborate" with "U.S. monopolies in their operations in Indonesia in the form of joint ventures." Aidit maintained that this

[60] *Harian Rakjat,* April 29, 1965.
[61] *Harian Rakjat,* May 7, 1965, in JPRS, *Translations on South and East Asia,* 92 (August 9, 1965): 19–20.
[62] *Harian Rakjat* editorial, May 10, 1965.

policy, administered in part by Charul Saleh, was out of step
with Sukarno's call for Indonesian self-reliance:

> The shortcoming of the people's actions in 1964 was the in-
> sufficient attack on the bureaucratic capitalists who serve as the
> center of the counterrevolution at home. Therefore, in 1965
> more actions must be launched demanding the retooling of all
> bureaucratic capitalists from all state apparatuses.[63]

Reflecting PKI successes through unilateral action initiated
by party mass organizations, Aidit's report cited the efficacy
of mass actions for political ends. They were developing a
"bigger and more decisive role [for] the masses in community
life and state policy." Aidit asserted that "our present
domestic and foreign policies are formed not only by our
state leaders" but also by the "masses [through] street demonstrations, the takeover of foreign enterprises at plantations,
oil fields, and factories." Although the PKI's agrarian actions
were ripening, Aidit considered that they had not yet matured. He gave warning that the party was prepared to
escalate its demand from simple reform to outright revolution in the countryside:

> As to the extent of these actions, they do not yet cover half
> the villages, . . . and are still limited to the demand for lower
> rents or a larger share of the crop. In other words, they are not
> actions to sweep aside the vestiges of feudalism. The test faced
> by the party today is to bring the antifeudal actions into step
> with anti-imperialist actions.

As a new means of influencing the countryside, Aidit urged
that party schools be established for the peasantry which
would develop their "political consciousness [through] the
mass education of Marxism among the peasants." Sensing
a propitious time to renew demands for a NASAKOM

---

[63] Aidit, *Report to Fourth Plenum*, May 11–13, 1965.

government, Aidit underlined the necessity for "retooling and NASAKOMization of the state apparatus," particularly those regional heads who have obstructed the party's agrarian agitation. If the president himself will not initiate "retooling" procedures, Aidit suggested, local elections should be held in order to correct the composition of government bodies which "no longer reflect the true balance among the political forces that exist in society." [64]

Indicative of the importance attached by Peking to the favorable PKI prospect was the delegation sent by the CCP to the party's May anniversary celebration in 1965. Led by Peng Chen, it included central committee members Liu Ning-I, Chen Yu, Wang Li, and Chang Shang-ming, a group probably equipped to carry out authoritative discussions with the PKI on its prognosis for future developments in the country. The Chinese press carried Sukarno's May 23 address to the party in which the president enthused: "The government of the Indonesian republic embraces the PKI . . . a tremendous factor in carrying on the Indonesian revolution." At the same time, however, Sukarno admitted that his leverage on the army was limited in implementing NASAKOM. Thus, he excluded the army from those groups needing to change their attitudes: "There are indeed persons who suffer communist phobia among the nationalists, there are persons suffering communist phobia among the religious believers, and *there were persons suffering communist phobia in the armed forces in the past.*" (Emphasis added.)

Chinese media also disseminated Aidit's reply to Sukarno in which he noted that "the portrait of Sukarno is hanging together with those of Marx, Engels, Lenin, and Stalin." [65] He also reminded his audience that the PKI was "the third

---

[64] NCNA, May 17, 1965, carried a summary of Aidit's report, highlighting his appeal for the NASAKOMization of the state apparatus, the development of the peasant movement, and general elections.
[65] NCNA dispatches on regional PKI celebrations mentioned the display of Mao's portrait too.

largest communist party in the world and the largest outside
the socialist camp." This strength "in accordance with the
NASAKOM theory of Bung Karno," Aidit continued, should
lead to "the realization of NASAKOM in all fields as the
absolute condition for the defense and development of political sovereignty." That the PKI had been convinced of
Sukarno's good faith even earlier was evidenced by the fact
that the July 1964 PKI National Conference had included as
background material the works of President Sukarno along
with those of Aidit, Lukman, Sakirman, and Bokri.[66]

Chinese congratulatory messages to the PKI nourished the
party's pride of place. Mao's note praised the party's achievements as a "glorious page . . . in the annals of revolution
in the East" because the PKI has "creatively applied and
developed Marxism-Leninism in the light of the revolutionary practice in its own country." [67] Peng Chen offered similar
accolades in his two speeches by attributing "the rapid
growth and brilliant achievements of the PKI" to the party's
success "at creatively integrating the universal truth of Marxism-Leninism with the concrete practices of Indonesian revolution." [68]

Underlining the rural predominance of Indonesian society,
Chinese treatment of the anniversary stressed the importance
of peasant support for future PKI actions. Peng Chen, for
example, noted approvingly that the PKI "attaches vital
importance to its work among the peasants" and "will prove
invincible as long as it rallies the overwhelming majority of
the peasants around it and exercises correct and firm leadership." [69] Chinese media carried Aidit's encouragement to
PKI youth to become "the right hand for the peasants'
struggle . . . to go to the countryside and up to the moun-

---

[66] *Harian Rakjat,* July 9, 1964, in JPRS, *Translations on South and East Asia,*
59 (August 7, 1964): 2.
[67] NCNA, May 22, 1965.
[68] *Ibid.,* May 27 and 30, 1965.
[69] *Ibid.*

tains." [70] NCNA reports of provincial celebrations commented that "the PKI had combined itself better with the peasants and adopted the method of eating together, living together, and working together." [71]

Rounding out what to the Chinese and the PKI must have appeared a near-perfect event, Sukarno capped his endorsement of the PKI with a renewed attack on the West, which could be equaled in vitriolic content only by those of the CPR. Speaking to the "NASAKOM cadres training course," Sukarno stated: "Imperialism could carry on peaceful coexistence with Moscow to some extent, but the Indonesian revolution cannot peacefully coexist with imperialism." Earlier Sukarno had declared, "Indonesia and China are carrying on a common struggle against all forms of imperialism. . . . The line of struggle of Indonesia and China is the same." [72] Liu Ning-I made a similar point on a visit to Lampung province, adding that imperialism was headed by their "common enemy . . . the United States." [73] And Peng Chen in Surabaya maintained that "Indonesia's heroic act of opposing imperialism has shaken the world. Imperialists headed by the United States and their lackeys unanimously hate you and are also afraid of you at the same time. . . . They are nothing but paper tigers. . . . The two peoples and two countries of China and Indonesia are intimate comrades-in-arms in the struggle against imperialism." [74]

THE PKI's GAMBIT FOR PARAMILITARY CAPABILITY

Although the public postures of the PKI and Sukarno seemed to denote a position of preeminence for the former by 1965, in actuality, the party had been unable to remedy

[70] *Ibid.*, May 25, 1965.
[71] *Ibid.*, June 2, 1965.
[72] *Ibid.*, May 25, 1965.
[73] *Ibid.*, May 29, 1965.
[74] *Ibid.*, May 30, 1965.

two basic weaknesses. First of all, it had been unsuccessful in its attempts to penetrate the bureaucracy, which meant that the party possessed virtually no patronage to use in recruiting among educated Indonesians. The party's mass base was not supplemented, then, by any effective penetration of the other levels of the Indonesian government. Hence in 1964, when the PKI stepped up its drive to retool the bureaucracy, it was, in effect, admitting its inability to manipulate governmental machinery in any other manner. The party had apparently opted for a campaign of stressing class antagonisms in the countryside to recruit the alienated at the cost of the horizontal support of more conservative groups like the military. Aidit may well have calculated that Sukarno's personal strength could offset military opposition. The party's second basic weakness grew out of this decision— its failure to offset the army's adamant opposition to its domestic activities. The army, in its capacity as regional administrator, found itself increasingly confronted with PKI-backed agitation after *Konfrontasi* began. Its predictable response was a combination of localized suppression and the creation of groups to rival such PKI fronts as the BTI and SOBSI.

That the Soviet-equipped army opposed PKI agitation without any apparent adverse reactions from Moscow was undoubtedly noted by both Peking and the PKI.[75] Indeed, it may not have been coincidental that the PKI's own campaign for radical agrarian action, which was so different from its posture of the 1950's and early 1960's, was roughly contemporaneous with such major CCP policy pronouncements of 1965 as the two statements on the Stalin question and the preceding CCP's Eighth National Congress, which had re-

[75] Tetsui Yashuhira, "Soviet Economic Aid to Nonaligned Countries," in Kurt London, ed., *New Nations in a Divided World* (New York: Frederick A. Praeger, 1963), p. 216.

jected the "parliamentary path" in favor of "revolutionary
struggle" outside the electoral process. The Chinese specifically called upon "proletarian parties" to "train their own
class forces." [76]

By early 1963, Aidit had pinpointed "economic and financial mismanagement" of the army's "bureaucratic capitalists"
as a major obstacle in the party's road to power. "Retooling"
these personnel became a major party goal even before the
inauguration of *Konfrontasi*.[77] In 1964, the PKI tested military resistance by initiating actions in rural Java through
its front organizations, SOBSI and BTI, against American
estates as well as both public and private landholdings. When
localized military resistance was countermanded by Sukarno,
the party assumed it had the green light to launch a full-
scale campaign for the unilateral implementation of the
1960 Agrarian Law and Law on Crop-sharing Agreements.
The party realized, however, that without a paramilitary
capability of its own, the military could move against it at
any time or place or whenever Sukarno's whim might change.

In order to protect and assist its rural agitators, Aidit proposed to provide arms to the peasantry in December 1964.
It is likely that Peking was consulted about this new policy,
for Chinese media provided complete coverage for Aidit's
mid-January 1965 appeal to Sukarno "to arm organized Indonesian workers and peasants" (controlled by PKI mass organizations), ostensibly in response to the British buildup in
Malaysia. Particularly noteworthy is the fact that Peking
continued publicizing Aidit's proposal even after Sukarno
had reportedly rejected it.[78] It is certainly conceivable that
the arming of PKI-controlled peasant groups was discussed
during Subandrio's late January visit to Peking during which

[76] See the discussion in Hinton, *China In World Politics*, p. 82.
[77] Aidit, *Dare, Dare, and Dare Again!* pp. 14–17.
[78] See NCNA, January 18 and 20, 1965; the *People's Daily* Observer article,
January 22, 1965; and the NCNA pickup of a BTI appeal, February 2, 1965.

Chinese leaders declared that relations between the two states had been elevated to a "new stage."

Growing reservations on the part of the army toward the Malaysian campaign were apparent in early 1965 when military leaders realized that the PKI was trying to capitalize on confrontation to press for an independent paramilitary capability.[79] By spring, Aidit had actually proposed the establishment of political commissars in the army, whose purpose would be to neutralize anti-communist officers. General Yani specifically rejected this proposal at an Armed Forces Seminar on April 8, stating that the army itself was a "shareholder wholly obligated to guarantee the progress of the Revolution" and not just a passive instrument of state.

In effect, the army had picked up the anti-communist cudgel where the BPS press had been forced to drop it in late 1964. The polemic continued through the respective presses of each side, with Peking frequently publicizing PKI demands for the arming of "organized" workers and peasants.[80] The army, for its part, continued to insist on the autonomy of the military as a political entity and on the right to determine its own composition: "ABRI has from the very beginning been NASAKOM, both in spirit and character. It is erroneous to believe that ABRI is still to be NASAKOMized." [81] The intensity of PKI–army opposition increased into the summer as the BTI linked its unilateral actions with appeals to arm the countryside, and various figures in the government such as Air Force Commander Dhani and Foreign Minister Subandrio took the party side. Peking duly reported all of these developments.[82]

[79] Frederick Bunnell, " 'Konfrontasi' and Indonesia" (paper prepared for the Meeting of the Association for Asian Studies, Chicago, March, 1967).
[80] See, for example, the dissemination of PKI slogans by NCNA, May 17, 1965.
[81] *Angatan Bersendjata,* May 18, 1965.
[82] See NCNA, June 24, July 20, and September 7, 1965.

Peking went further than mere media endorsement of PKI demands as Sukarno revealed on May 31 that Chou En-lai had supported the PKI's proposals soon after they were initiated.[83] Apparently, Sukarno's revelation of high-level Chinese endorsement of PKI demands and his willingness to reconsider his earlier refusal to supply arms to the peasantry elicited more adamant objections from the military. By the summer of 1965, army leaders felt compelled to reject explicitly any "structure of political commissars" for the army; going further, they even publicly objected to PKI unilateral peasant actions and the party's apparent control of the Indonesian news agency Antara.[84] It also seems likely that army leaders were exercised by Sukarno's January CBS-TV interview during which he accepted the prospects of PKI accession with complete equanimity.[85]

Reinforcing the CPR's earlier endorsement of PKI mass actions, Peng Chen pressed the importance of a peasant base during his visit for the forty-fifth party anniversary: "The party of the working class," he instructed, "will prove invincible as long as it rallies the overwhelming majority of the peasants around it and exercises correct and firm leadership." [86] At the climax of his stay, Peng Chen offered the first open, high-level Peking endorsement of the PKI's request to arm the peasants in his address of May 27. Peking also reported Aidit's renewed "demand" for arms in which he stated that he was convinced that only "armed workers and peasants can halt the invasion by imperialist troops. . . . The struggle of the Vietnamese people is a vivid proof of this truth." [87]

---

[83] J. O. Sutter, "Two Faces of 'Konfrontasi': Crush Malaysia and the 'Gestapu,'" *Asian Survey* (October, 1966), p. 536.

[84] See *Angatan Bersendjata,* June 29–July 1, 1965, and Radio Free Europe Research Department, *The PKI and the Army,* vol. 85 (August 11, 1965).

[85] Cited in Brackman, *Southeast Asia's Second Front,* p. 102.

[86] NCNA, May 27, 1965.

[87] *Ibid.,* May 23, 1965.

The PKI moved to counteract army opposition by increasing its own pressure on Sukarno to "retool [the] bureaucratic capitalists." In his May political report, Aidit urged: "In 1965 we should work harder at actions demanding the resignation of bureaucratic capitalists from all government services, plants, and commercial enterprises."[88] To enhance its drive against the army, the PKI tried to convince Sukarno that the military was plotting a coup against him. In a May Politburo statement the party charged "bureaucratic capitalists" with "trying to grab political power through a *coup d'état.*" [89]

Reminiscent of Peng Chen's remarks in May, the Peking press in June highlighted those sections of Aidit's political report criticizing bureaucratic capitalists, demanding their removal from state organs and encouraging intensified mass actions and the arming of workers and peasants. In the report Aidit argued for the efficacy of mass actions on state policy:

> Our present domestic and foreign policies are formed not only by our state leaders. The Indonesian people's masses also are actively and consciously forming our domestic and foreign policies through actions such as street demonstrations, the takeover of foreign enterprises . . . oil fields, and in peasant mass actions for the destruction of village devils.[90]

Aidit apparently hoped to win over the armed forces in the rural areas to the PKI's cause, for "the armed forces of the Indonesian republic . . . are nothing more than armed peasants." Sukarno implicitly backed most of Aidit's demands in his August 17, 1965, Independence Day address (with Chen I as an honored guest), an address prepared with PKI Second Deputy Chairman Njoto's assistance according to testimony

[88] Aidit, *Report to Fourth Plenum,* May 11, 1965, in JPRS, p. 21.
[89] PKI Central Committee Politburo Statement, May 7, 1965, in JPRS, *Translations on South and East Asia,* p. 7.
[90] *People's Daily,* June 12, 1965.

at Subandrio's trial in October 1966. Opposing the army,
Sukarno for the second time stated his support of a policy
to arm workers and peasants (the "Fifth Force") and spoke
once again of a foreign policy axis consisting of the Asian
bloc, Indonesia, and Cambodia.[91] One observer reported that
upon Sukarno's August endorsement of the "Fifth Force,"
Subandrio made arrangements for surreptitious small arms
shipments from Peking, which presumably found their way
into PKI hands, since SOBSI workers handled the unload-
ing.[92] It is certainly conceivable that the PKI feared the
prospect of a preemptive army coup after Sukarno's August
endorsement of most party stands and asked for Chinese
arms either to forestall such an action or, as a last resort, to
beat it to the punch.[93]

Aidit was elated with Sukarno's August statement that
"Indonesia will build socialism when imperialist capital is
finished and the land belonging to the landlords is returned
to the people." This was almost an exact reiteration of the
PKI's two-stage revolution, to which Aidit added that Sukarno's speech proved that the PKI was not revisionist because Sukarno followed the party, not vice versa.[94]

Subandrio, always able to move with the trend of events,
interpreted Sukarno's August address as a full endorsement
of the communist party. He followed suit by seconding
Aidit's call for the removal of bureaucratic capitalists. The
PKI's Pemuda Rakjat picked up Subandrio's endorsement
and declared that it "should be interpreted by youths as an
order to launch mass and revolutionary actions throughout
the country [against] corrupters and kabir [to] drag them

[91] Phnom Penh was less than enthusiastic about Sukarno's axis and demonstrated its independence in August by recognizing Singapore's secession from
Malaysia, when no other member of the erstwhile "axis" so acted.
[92] Sutter, "Two Faces of 'Konfrontasi,'" p. 536.
[93] See Dommen, "Attempted Coup in Indonesia," p. 155.
[94] *Harian Rakjat*, August 21, 1965, in JPRS, *Translations on South and East
Asia*, 98 (October 13, 1965): 3–4.

to the gallows or to be shot in public." On September 25, less than a week prior to the coup attempt, Sukarno stated in a speech to a PKI student group: "We are now about to enter the second stage of the Indonesian revolution, namely implementation of socialism." He also pointed out that certain generals who were resisting the revolution might have to be eliminated.[95] Just three days later, Peking reported Aidit's exhortation to Indonesian workers to take over control of state-run enterprises from bureaucratic capitalists who are "counterrevolutionaries and must be wiped out." [96]

At the same time the PKI Estates Workers Union seemed so self-confident that it was agitating for the dismissal of specific individuals from government companies. In a speech to the union conference, Aidit urged not only a "struggle for a portion of salted fish, but also toward political power. . . . Dare, act, and move against the devils of the cities, that is, the high and mighty, thieves and corrupters." [97] As a final bold jab at the government, Aidit even went so far as to criticize Sukarno's cabinet appointments, labeling them men of "absolutely no political stature" who survive through a "ration of political stature . . . from Bung Karno." [98] As if in almost complete agreement with the party, Sukarno, in a speech at a PKI student conference the day before the coup, explained that he had ordered all Indonesian government agencies to dismiss any employee who is not "progressive-revolutionary." [99] The PKI confidently predicted that "the rise of a NASAKOM cabinet cannot be prevented, not even by the Seventh Fleet nor, as Bung Karno said, *by the moron in a general's uniform.*" (Emphasis added.)[100]

[95] Quoted in Dommen, "Attempted Coup in Indonesia," p. 538.
[96] NCNA, September 28, 1965.
[97] *Harian Rakjat,* September 27, 1965, in JPRS, *Translations on South and East Asia,* 99 (October 26, 1965): 71, 76.
[98] *Ibid.,* p. 77.
[99] Djakarta Domestic Service, September 30, 1965.
[100] *Harian Rakjat,* September 29, 1965, in JPRS, *Translations on South and East Asia,* 106 (December 13, 1965): 19.

By the time of the coup, Sukarno and his entourage had consciously or unconsciously so changed their value structure from their early claim to legitimacy that they had, in effect, lost that claim to lead the revolution. The Indonesian revolution, initiated to achieve the nationalist goal of political identity, had been metamorphosed into the PKI's conception of revolution which in turn was highly colored by the CCP model. When opposition to the revolution became synonymous with opposition to the PKI, anti-communist forces in Indonesia had no option but resistance, a choice quite clearly exercised in the aftermath of the coup.[101]

[101] See the perceptive discussion in Weatherbee, *Ideology in Indonesia*, p. 97.

6

The Triangle Breaks: Post-Coup Deterioration
of Sino-Indonesian Relations

In the first part of this study I tried to analyze both the internal and foreign policy determinants leading to the creation of a Sino-Indonesian alliance in the first half of the 1960's. Relying on qualitative content analysis of the Peking, PKI, and, to a limited extent, the noncommunist Djakarta press, I focused on the mutual perceptions of the three major actors and the probable connections between these perceptions and their political actions toward one another. I shall now examine the affect of changing mutual perceptions on the breakdown of the alliance as a new military elite rose to power in Indonesia. In addition to applying qualitative content analysis to the post-October 1965 Sino-Indonesian relationship, I shall also develop some semiquantitative data presentations to expose the communications pattern between the two states as the alliance became disrupted. These presentations will illustrate not just a change in the frequency of transactions but, more importantly, the quality of these transactions, namely, from positive to negative.

In effect, I shall be decomposing a macrosituation—the breakdown of the Sino-Indonesian alliance—into some of its subprocesses, particularly the frequency and substance of communications-flows, relating the patterns of these flows to the political behavior of the actors. We are *not*, then, concerned with explicating the coup itself as a dependent variable; that is, trying to isolate the independent variables which could account for the *actual* event.[1] Rather, we shall accept the coup as a major independent variable and examine its impact on Sino-Indonesian relations and the shattered aspirations of the PKI.

Within a week after the coup attempt, ostensibly led by middle-level army officers in the president's palace guard, the internal Indonesian power ratio had drastically changed. The conservative anti-communist officer corps centered around Suharto and Nasution came to the fore, to the detriment of the PKI's representatives and sympathizers who had been either killed or arrested, or were in hiding, or, in the case of Njoto, were simply bypassed in the decision-making process. Suharto and Nasution were creating a new government, a government faced with violent insurrection, for which a scapegoat had to be found. The PKI fitted the bill perfectly as the new military government amplified the already considerable circumstantial evidence implicating the party. The military press, for example, publicized the *Harian Rakjat* article of October 2 endorsing the discredited coup as well as the fact that prominent PKI members were among those listed in the October 1 announcement of the Revolutionary Council. The scapegoating technique which the PKI had employed with such effectiveness against the military bureaucracy in the pre-coup period to displace the frustration-aggression syndrome in Indonesian political life was now

[1] Of the few informed analyses to date, by far the best are Arthur J. Dommen, "The Attempted Coup in Indonesia," *China Quarterly* (January–March, 1966), and J. O. Sutter, "Two Faces of 'Konfrontasi': Crush Malaysia and the 'Gestapu,'" *Asian Survey* (October, 1966). For a dissenting view which argues that the coup was really an internal army affair between the Diponegaro Division and the Djakarta-based Supreme Command, see W. F. Wertheim, "Indonesia Before and After the Untung Coup," *Pacific Affairs*, 39, nos. 1, 2 (Spring–Summer, 1966).

reversed by the military with even more telling results. This technique was used at first just against the PKI, but soon thereafter it was used as well against the large Overseas Chinese community in Indonesia which was depicted as Peking's "fifth column."[2] The bloodbath that followed during the next nine months was unprecedented in Indonesia in its ferocity. As one observer put it: "The dead outnumbered the toll at Hiroshima by a third, were more than all those killed on both sides in Vietnam since the fight began against the French 15 years ago."[3]

The PKI did not rescind its endorsement of the coup until October 6, perhaps because of a breakdown in party communications since the leadership was either scattered or decimated. Even then, the Central Committee released a weak statement reiterating that the coup was an internal army affair and that the PKI members listed on the Revolutionary Council had "not [been] notified or had not given their approval." Lukman and Njoto similarly stated to Djakarta newsmen that the PKI did not support the coup, despite earlier *Harian Rakjat* articles to the contrary. Testimony introduced over one year later at former Foreign Minister Subandrio's military trial suggested, however, not only that the PKI had supported and helped to plan the coup but also that high-level officials around Sukarno knew of the plan and of PKI clandestine training activities.[4] Further testimony at the later trial of PKI member Sudisman indicated that the PKI discussed the formation of a revolutionary council in late August to forestall any action by the "Council of Gen-

[2] The Indonesian coup case fits the Feierabend's conceptual categories of political frustration-aggression theory very closely. See I. K. and R. L. Feierabend, "Aggressive Behaviors Within Polities, 1948–1962: A Cross-National Study," *Journal of Conflict Resolution*, 10, no. 3 (September, 1966): 251–56.

[3] Horace Sutton, "Indonesia's Night of Terror," *Saturday Review*, February 4, 1967, p. 27.

[4] See the testimony in *Duta Masjarakat*, October 26, 1966, in JPRS, *Translations on South and East Asia*, December 27, 1966, p. 37.

erals" which the party claimed was planning its own coup. According to Sudisman, the meeting authorized the creation of a Pemuda Rakjat "reserve force" to be trained at the air force training ground in Lubangbuaja.[5]

Djakarta reports of Njono's written testimony intimate that the PKI Politburo decided on a coup around the end of July after Aidit reported on the president's illness and the favorable prospects for support from "progressive officers" in the military. The timing suggests the possibility of Chinese involvement because Aidit had also flown to Peking in July, probably to discuss Sukarno's illness as diagnosed by Chinese doctors and the likely course of PKI actions. Thus it is probable that the CCP was apprised of PKI plans.[6] However, the final decision was not made until August 28, giving the party only a little over one month to prepare.[7] The only effective redoubts established for the party were in Central Java where party remnants sustained resistance until late December under local revolutionary councils.[8]

In any case, the PKI's actions during the abortive coup provided the military and Moslem organizations with enough circumstantial evidence to make a convincing popular (if not legal) case against the PKI. The military immediately charged the PKI with attempting a "second Madiun" and, within three days of the coup, had already begun a campaign to ban the party, engendering an atmosphere which encouraged harassment of all suspected party members as well as Overseas Chinese who, for the most part, had been organized by the PKI-controlled *Baperki*. It was common knowledge during the Sukarno era that Baperki had become a major channel of funds from the CPR to the PKI. Repressed hostility against the Overseas Chinese, which had accumulated during the

[5] Djakarta Domestic Service, July 6, 1967.
[6] See the discussion in Sutter, "Two Faces of 'Konfrontasi,' " p. 535.
[7] Djakarta Domestic Service, July 13, 1967.
[8] Sutter, "Two Faces of 'Konfrontasi,' " p. 542.

period they enjoyed Sukarno's protection, was suddenly released and encouraged by the military with a vengeance.[9]

Many observers were taken aback by the PKI's failure to resist military repression after the coup attempt, especially in light of its vaunted claims of a membership in the millions. While one explanation might well be inflated membership figures to enhance the party's domestic image in the pre-coup period, a more satisfactory one would have to include an assessment of the type of commitment held by party members. A recent theoretical study, which might well apply to the PKI case, has provided considerable insight into the nature of group commitment under stressful conditions. It is based on a set of hypotheses concerning the willingness of individuals in large groups voluntarily to risk their own interests for the advancement of group objectives. According to the hypotheses tested on American labor and agricultural groups, an individual will not voluntarily exert himself to help the group when he perceives a higher cost (or risk) to himself than the value which can be gained by the group or when he perceives that his individual effort would be meaningless. In algebraic terms, this proposition would be expressed:

If $Fi > C/Vg$, then the individual will act in the party's interest.

(Fi) the amount of the party's goal enjoyed by the individual;

(C) the cost to the individual of working towards that goal—in the case of the coup, perhaps his life;

(Vg) the total value of the party's goal—in the case of the coup, control of the government.[10]

[9] Donald Kirk, "Indonesia's Chinese Are People without a Country," *New York Times Magazine,* October 23, 1966, p. 151.
[10] Mancur Olson, *The Logic of Collective Action: Public Goods and the Theory of Groups* (Cambridge, Mass.: Harvard University Press, 1965), pp. 23–24, 126–29.

In the PKI case, then, it seems reasonable to hypothesize that since the party relied on mass *voluntaristic* support, in case of a showdown, such support would be withdrawn because the risk to individuals involved would be perceived as greater than both the potential payoff of party success and the likelihood of the party ever achieving that success. Thus, the PKI organization in the post-coup period, with exceptions in the traditional party stronghold of Central Java, rapidly disintegrated as *individuals* acted to sever their ties with the party.

Ruth McVey, fully two years before the coup, presciently described what was to occur in October 1965. Drawing an analogy between the PKI of the 1960's and the CCP of the 1920's, with Sukarno as Sun Yat-sen and Nasution as Chiang Kai-shek, she speculated that if a Shanghai occurred in Indonesia, the PKI would not be so fortunate as the CCP, for the islands would provide no Yenan.[11]

THE DESTRUCTION OF PEKING'S ALLIANCE PLANS

Perhaps the greatest paradox of the coup lay in its destruction of the Sino-Indonesian alliance just as it had reached an apex of solidarity. According to Subandrio during his October 1966 trial, after Indonesia withdrew from the United Nations, the government elicited a CPR promise that it would assist Indonesia in case of attack by either the United States or Britain.[12] By moving unsuccessfully against the military, the PKI succeeded in destroying what Sukarno and the Chinese government had been creating over a period of several years. Contrary to its militant call for the overthrow of bourgeois governments, Peking, perhaps accepting the PKI's assessment of Sukarno as "pro-people," had pursued a "right strategy" toward Djakarta by collaborating with the

[11] Ruth T. McVey, "Indonesian Communism and the Transition to Guided Democracy," in A. Doak Barnett, ed., *Communist Strategies in Asia* (New York: Frederick A. Praeger, 1963), p. 188.
[12] Djakarta Domestic Service, October 17, 1966.

Indonesian government and acquiescing in a united front from above in which the PKI was only one, not the leading, factor. The PKI had gone so far as to declare that the Liu Shao-chi–Aidit 1963 exchange of visits had "consolidated still more the bridge of Indonesian-Chinese friendship erected by President Sukarno." [13] In other words, Aidit was merely acting as Sukarno's agent in promoting Sino-Indonesian relations.

The flustered and hesitant reaction of the Chinese to the coup may have mirrored either suprise at its occurrence or surprise at its rapid and total failure. Although the Chinese press did not report the coup attempt until October 19, there were indications that something was amiss as early as the third when Chou En-lai and Liu Shao-chi dispatched a message to Sukarno stating: "We have learned from the radio broadcasts from Djakarta that Your Excellency the President is in good health, and we hereby extend to you cordial regards and heartfelt wishes." A terse NCNA item the next day remarked only that Sukarno had left Djakarta "owing to a sudden domestic incident." Peking media also disseminated a statement by the leaders of the parliamentary and other Indonesian delegations visiting China for its anniversary celebrations which pledged in connection with "the latest political situation" at home that they would remain faithful to Sukarno's leadership "in whatever circumstances." [14] Apparently, at this point when the coup's fortunes had faded but not entirely disappeared, Peking had decided to express its continued support for Sukarno in hopes that whatever the outcome he could salvage the PKI's position and the Sino-Indonesian relationship. This impression was reinforced when Peking also carried the greeting of General Nasution, who at that time was mobilizing an all-out campaign to hunt

[13] Cited in Arnold C. Brackman, "The Malay World and China," in A. M. Halpern, ed., Policies Toward China (New York: McGraw-Hill, 1966), p. 282.
[14] NCNA, October 4, 1965.

down the PKI, wishing "that existing good relations between the armed forces of the CPR and the Indonesian Republic [would] continue to grow." [15]

Meanwhile the CPR continued its formal negotiations with visiting Indonesian delegations as though nothing had happened. A joint communiqué between parliamentary representatives of the two countries conveyed the first official Chinese endorsement of the Djakarta-formulated, Asian revolutionary axis: "The Chinese side holds that the Djakarta–Phnom Penh–Hanoi–Peking–Pyongyang axis of anti-imperialist struggle, which was proposed by President Sukarno, reflects the will of the people of the above-mentioned countries to strength their mutual solidarity and to unite with other people for the common cause of opposing imperialism." [16] Concurrent events proved this statement, desired for so long by Sukarno, to be a hollow mockery.

Sukarno undoubtedly reciprocated China's initial hopes that despite the coup's outcome relations between the two states would remain close. He said as much in an October 27 interview with the Chinese ambassador when it had become apparent that the PKI was being decimated. By then, however, the Chinese had switched their strategy, as Subandrio confirmed when he admitted that the Chinese aid program had been stopped. [17]

As to Peking's complicity in the initial coup action, the evidence is mixed. It seems unlikely that Peking would have risked its state relations with Indonesia unless it was convinced that a military coup was imminent. Accepting the latter premise, the British historian H. R. Trevor-Roper, who was in Peking at the time of the coup, had the impression that the Chinese took credit for Gestapu as soon as it occurred by reporting it to foreign visitors, though not to the Chinese

[15] *Ibid.*, October 8, 1965.
[16] *Ibid.*, October 7, 1965.
[17] Cited in Dommen, "Attempted Coup in Indonesia," p. 155.

public, "in circumstances which clearly indicated a deliberate policy, determined on high." [18] Only three weeks before the coup, the Chinese reported a major address given by Aidit at the PKI's peasant academy in which he exhorted: "Genuine revolutionaries are not afraid of sustaining any losses because of revolution. . . . Marxism teaches us that socialism . . . must be realized by way of revolution." [19] This speech was delivered after the Politburo allegedly made its coup plans in late August.

Peking's long public silence on the coup probably reflected the fluidity of events in Indonesia and Chinese hopes that the PKI could somehow salvage its position. When it became apparent that such a prospect was extremely unlikely, Chinese media published a long roundup of events on October 19 and 20, presenting their interpretations of "the sudden drastic political changes in the Indonesian situation." While defending the PKI's position shifts of the preceding weeks, the roundup had the effect of implicating the Indonesian party in the coup attempt by reporting both its initial support of the Revolutionary Council on October 2 and then its disassociation from it three days later as "an internal affair of the army" in which the PKI "would not intervene." Peking deplored the military arrests of "communists and other progressives" and attacks on PKI headquarters and mass organization affiliates.

It seems plausible in retrospect that Chinese officials had concluded as early as October 19 that Sukarno's position had been irreparably undermined by the anti-communist military around Suharto and Nasution in the post-coup period. The roundup, in effect, accused Sukarno of being unable to defend the PKI against a military crackdown and of capitulating to military demands. In its chronology of develop-

---

[18] H. R. Trevor-Roper, "Understanding Mao, or Look Back to Stalin," *New York Times Magazine,* February, 12, 1967.
[19] NCNA, September 7, 1965.

ments, the Chinese media noted the following order of events:

(1) Sukarno announced he was in command of the situation and appointed Major General Ranoto Reksosamudro (a leftist officer) to take temporary charge of routine army affairs;

(2) Major General Suharto took control of Djakarta, and Radio Djakarta announced that he had taken over actual command of the army;

(3) Sukarno then publicly assigned responsibility to Suharto for restoring order, while reaffirming Reksosamudro as army commander;

(4) and finally, after an army-instituted reign of terror against the PKI, Sukarno on October 14 named Suharto commander and "relieved Reksosamudro of the post to which Sukarno himself had appointed him on 1 October." Suharto, in turn, declared he "had Sukarno's trust."

The roundup also carried Peking's first reports of Indonesian anti-China demonstrations, tying them into moves against the PKI. Peking charged anti-PKI agitators with distributing "anti-China leaflets . . . under instructions" which accused the CPR of "stage-managing the September 30 movement."

Polemical overtones were also present in the roundup, which charged *Izvestiya* with tacitly approving the anti-PKI campaign when it accused *Harian Rakjat* of the mistake of writing "as if the rebellion had the support of the people." As for the CPR interpretation of the coup, Peking presaged its own later comment by reprinting an analysis from the pro-Peking, New Zealand communist party organ, *People's Voice*, which asserted that the military coup resulted from an American CIA plot to establish a "military dictatorship," and that the PKI has "never fallen victim to the illusions spread by revisionists that the transition to socialism can be accomplished peacefully." [20]

On November 5, Chinese media printed the second installment of their interpretation of Indonesian developments. The new materials sharpened Peking's earlier portrayal of Sukarno as an ineffectual captive of the army who had sold out the PKI "under various pressures." Although Sukarno is quoted as calling for an end to anti-China incidents, the second roundup goes on to detail their recurrence despite his pleas. The documentation of Sukarno's speeches highlighted his capitulation to the military's version of the coup, noting that "he does not consider the September 30 incident right," that he regarded it as "very wrong" and "will punish" its instigators. At the same time, the roundup reiterated the PKI position of noninvolvement in the September 30 "affair," although considering it "correct." In the Chinese account, Subandrio was portrayed as sharing Sukarno's opportunism. He is quoted as branding the coup attempt "counterrevolutionary" and insisting that Sukarno will "definitely punish the criminals," and that "we will be firm with the CPR as well if necessary."

The Chinese also pictured Sukarno and his entourage as ineffective in their efforts to put "an end to activities to whip up hatred against China." Despite Sukarno's injunction, Peking charged, Indonesian army units abetted by "right wing papers" have been engaged in a "systematic and organized undermining" of "Overseas Chinese organizations and personal property." The report noted pointedly that each appeal by Sukarno for a halt to these depredations was followed by new outbursts.

Peking seemed to be laying the groundwork for a change of policy toward both Indonesia and Sukarno. Later Chinese reports on the Indonesian situation, however, indicated that

[20] *Ibid.*, October 21, 1965.

there may still have been disagreement within the Chinese hierarchy concerning Sukarno's usefulness if he could at least salvage his own position and prestige from the leftist debacle. In reporting Sukarno's November 6 cabinet address, Chinese media underlined his insistence on retaining crypto-communist Oie Tjoe Tat in the cabinet despite demands by "some people" bent on turning "this revolution of ours to the Right." Although reporting his praise for the CPR, passages from his address were also included which intimated that he might, under army pressure, ban the PKI: "Some people have urged me to dissolve the PKI. I am giving consideration to all questions related to the dissolution of the PKI." Sukarno also contradicted the PKI's October 5 declaration that the September 30 movement was an internal army affair by maintaining that it was "not merely a problem of the army," but a "national problem, a political problem." [21]

As November wore on the CPR probably became increasingly convinced that Sukarno was losing his power to protect both the PKI and Overseas Chinese from the military. Peking, for example, reported General Suharto's rectification directive issued under Sukarno's name, which, in effect, gave the army power to purge all civilian and military organs of those who were "implicated in the September 30 movement," including "members of the PKI." [22] The next day Peking announced the first outright dissolution of a regional PKI chapter in West Java on orders from the regional military commander.[23] By decentralizing its anti-communist campaign, the military had succeeded in removing it from Sukarno's control.

Peking's summarization of the Soviet press in the postcoup period elucidated the polemical dimension of its Indonesian policy. Searing the October 26 *Pravda* editorial

[21] *Ibid.*, November 17, 1965.
[22] *Ibid.*, November 18, 1965.
[23] *Ibid.*, November 19, 1965.

article for indirectly accusing the PKI of "political adventurism, putschism, and sectarianism," Peking inferred that the U.S.S.R. was secretly applauding the destruction of the PKI and that, despite the changed nature of the Indonesian government, "the Soviet Union has given and continues to give all-out assistance and support to the Republic of Indonesia." [24] China's European spokesman, Albania, went even further by accurately insisting that it was Soviet military assistance which gave the Indonesian army the wherewithal to destroy the PKI.[25]

Despite Peking's decision to lay a good share of the blame for the PKI defeat at Sukarno's feet, the Indonesian president tried to preserve and protect some variant of the Indonesian Communist Party, first by proposing that a "loyal" party be formed and then, as late as February 1966, insisting that the PKI had made many glorious contributions to the onward march of the Indonesian revolution.[26]

By the end of 1966, the Sino-Indonesian informal alliance had been irrevocably broken. The rapidity of its destruction, which will be discussed in detail later, resulted from the fact that the system-ideology established between Sukarno, the PKI, and the CPR had never really been accepted by alternative power elites in Indonesia. Rather, these elites, particularly the military and Moslem groups, had viewed the alliance with considerable misgivings from the very beginning. They had gone along with Sukarno, in part because of his charismatic hold, and in part because of specific rewards inherent in the Bung's policy, such as high military budgets. But once the president was discredited and the military rose as an alternative power center, previously repressed conflicts between the CPR and Indonesia immediately resurfaced, most notably conflict over the status of the Overseas Chinese,

[24] *Ibid.*, November 5, 1965.
[25] *Zeri I Popullit,* November 4, 1965.
[26] Cited in Bernard K. Gordon, "Regionalism and Instability in Southeast Asia," *Orbis,* 10, no. 2 (Summer, 1966): 478–79.

who were viewed by Moslem groups as a perennial economic threat and by the military as a major source of PKI funds and a Communist Chinese Fifth Column. Although Sukarno had succeeded in the first half of the 1960's in papering over endemic Indonesian hostility to the resident Chinese, this hostility had not been dissipated. Since Sukarno was no longer able to control Indonesian animosity toward these Chinese, the military and Moslem groups could direct their ire against them in order to legitimize their own positions in the new political order.

The brutal slaughter of the army's general staff by the PKI youth and women's groups, a story disseminated in detail by the Indonesian radio and press, was interpreted by village Java as the ultimate affront against the country by a party which had become intimately associated with both the CPR and the Overseas Chinese. Waves of terror spread over the island and beyond, focusing particularly on the Overseas Chinese, who had become tied in the popular image with the assassination of the generals. In addition to this new grievance, behind the anti-Chinese terror was the Indonesian's traditional ethnic antagonism toward his more affluent Chinese neighbor. The resulting violence was not confined to the Indonesian peasant but, significantly, included regional officials of the same ethnic background. Thus, post-coup, anti-Chinese depredations received local official sanction.[27]

The appalling long-lived violence of the anti-China campaign in Indonesia—still proceeding at the time of this writing (December 1967)—can only be explained as a combination of deeply ingrained national prejudice and official policy. As we shall see, the CPR chose to ignore the former and stress the latter in its own reaction to the incarceration and slaughter of its nationals. For Indonesia, however, the

---

[27] Economic grievances between ethnic Indonesians and Chinese were reflected in the relative incomes of the two groups, the former earning roughly five per cent of the latter's annual income. See Kirk, "Indonesia's Chinese," p. 141.

campaign served both "safety-valve" and "scapegoating" functions. The post-coup military government consciously encouraged the anti-China campaign to deflect popular pressure
at least temporarily away from economic grievances and onto
a powerless target. Thus the Indonesian masses could release
pent-up tension accumulated against the total system by vent-
ing it on a powerless scapegoat community, the Overseas
Chinese. The community was powerless because its domestic
protectors, the PKI and Sukarno, had been discredited, and
the CPR, its external protector, because of its geographical
distance, could only fulminate ineffectually and, paradoxically, appeal to international law. As Lewis Coser succinctly
put it in accounting for the manifest violence of long-re-
pressed conflicts once they were unleashed: "If conflict breaks
out in a group that has consistently tried to prevent expression of hostile feelings, it will be particularly intense for two
reasons: First, because the conflict does not merely aim at re-
solving the immediate issue which led to its outbreak; all
accumulated grievances which were denied expression previously are apt to emerge at this occasion." [28] Coser's proposition helps to explain the beatings, murders, and looting to
which the Chinese in Indonesia were subject in the post-coup
period as economic, ethnic, and political grievances came
together.

PEKING'S REACTIONS TO POST-COUP,
ANTI-CHINESE DEPREDATIONS

Most of the remainder of this chapter is devoted to an assessment of the pattern of hostility exhibited by China in its
reaction to Indonesian developments from October 1965
through December 1967. We shall delineate the dimensions
of this pattern through graph and verbal analyses in hopes of
explaining both specific Chinese perceptions of the new anti-

[28] Lewis Coser, *The Functions of Social Conflict* (New York: Free Press of
Glencoe, 1956), p. 152.

TOTAL CHINESE ATTENTION TO INDONESIA IN THE POST-COUP PERIOD
(BASED ON THEME)
OCTOBER 1965–DECEMBER 1967

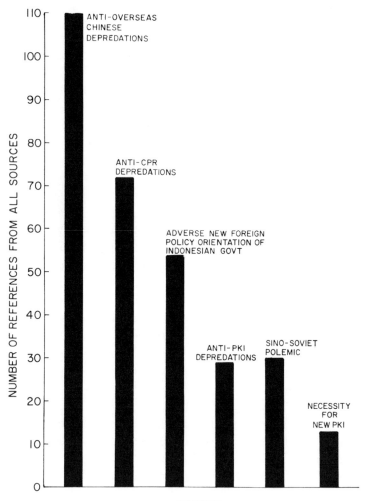

thetical relations with Indonesia and China's more general
world view insofar as that is also revealed in its articulated
estimation of Indonesia. Because of the large number of
documents included in the analysis, we shall not attempt to
provide a "blow-by-blow" account of Chinese recriminations.
Rather, we shall select specific verbal examples to illustrate
the graph presentations and to show the stages of development as relations between the two states moved from annoyance to bitter hostility. We shall see how different issues
and types of hostility were associated with specific stages in
the deteriorating relationship which at the least have led to
the cessation of all forms of interstate cooperation and at the
most could lead to the severance of diplomatic relations
along with Chinese support for a new PKI operating out of
Peking and perhaps even a government-in-exile.

The above figure thematically summarizes in graph form
all official Chinese protests to Indonesia as well as commen-
tary-length (at least 300 words) statements in national-level
Chinese media on Indonesian affairs. Some documents are
counted more than once when they include more than one
theme. However, these data in general understate total Chinese attention to Indonesia because they do not include
commentaries of less than 300 words, nor those in which a
major portion of the text (determined by the author) is not
devoted to Indonesia. The graph illustrates the major dimensions of China's concern with Indonesia.

The table on page 128 presents the same material, this time
broken down by source frequency. Both the graph and the
table illustrate China's manifest concern with the fate of
the resident Chinese in Indonesia and the dim prospects for
maintaining some effective Chinese diplomatic presence. Of
the total of 308 entries, 182 (or 59 per cent) are devoted to
either anti-CPR or anti-Overseas Chinese incidents. The next
highest dimension indicates concern over the radical change
in Indonesia's foreign policy orientation. The dates placed

Chinese Attitudes Toward Post-Coup Indonesia
Theme Analysis Table*
October 1965–December 1967
(N = 308)

Source	Anti-PKI Depredations	Anti-CPR Depredations	Sino-Soviet Polemic	Anti-Overseas Chinese Depredations	Adverse New Foreign Policy Orientation of Indonesian Government	Necessity for New PKI
CPR Foreign Ministry		26		11 (April '66)	1	
CPR Embassy		18	8	34	1	
People's Daily	2	5	1	8	12	
Liberation Army Daily	1	1				
NGNA and Other Press	21	20	15	43	36 (April '66)	9 (April '66)
Front Groups	5	2 (April '66)	6	14 (May '66)	4	4
Total	29	72	30	110	54	13 (June '66)
Theme						

* See text for explanation of table.

within certain of these dimensions specify the first time the theme appeared in a particular source. The date on the foreign policy dimension is noteworthy because it indicates a time lag of several months between the coup and Peking's decision to publicize its displeasure with Indonesia's new foreign policies under Suharto. The April 1966 date follows closely upon Sukarno's March 12 surrender of authority to Suharto, probably interpreted by Chinese leaders as a point of no return in state relations: It was only after this event that Chinese media also began publicizing the prospects for a revitalized Peking-based PKI.

All of these dimensions are multifactor in makeup. In the analysis to follow, I propose to discuss these factors in some detail, for only by such treatment can the meaning of these perceptual dimensions for Chinese policy be explicated. A convenient starting point is the CPR protest against attacks on its diplomatic establishment and against the atrocities committed against the Overseas Chinese.

The acknowledged seriousness of Indonesian depredations to the CPR is demonstrated by both its general attention to the problem (see Table 1) and, more specifically, by its official protests (see Figure 4 below). In the latter case, lower-level embassy notes are more frequently employed than high-level foreign ministry protests: however, the pattern of the two is roughly comparable except for the last six months in 1967 when the Chinese embassy was under a semi-permanent state of siege. The two peaks on the figure below occur in the April–June 1966 and April–June 1967 periods, both of which were times of widespread violence against resident Chinese and harassment of CPR diplomats who were trying to care for the interests of these people or make arrangements for their passage back to China.

A more detailed discussion of these protests illustrates the substance of China's complaints and its general inability to react effectually to the Indonesian challenge. The official

FREQUENCY OF CPR OFFICIAL PROTESTS TO INDONESIA IN THE POST-COUP PERIOD
(BY SOURCE)
OCTOBER 1965–DECEMBER 1967

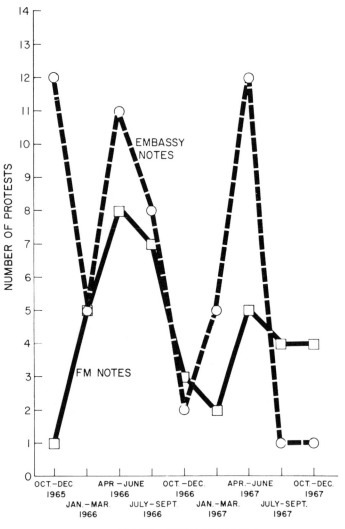

protests began just one day before the first NCNA roundup
of events in Indonesia on October 19. They comprised the
first official Chinese protests to Indonesia since the July 1960
anti-Chinese riots in Java. These initial complaints were directed at violation of the diplomatic immunity of Chinese
officials in Indonesia through "attack and search" of their
persons and premises. The first protest, at the foreign ministry level, declared that such actions "impaired the friendly
relations between China and Indonesia" and accused the
Indonesian government of "condoning" a stream of "lies
and slanders" about China from October 1, which was leading to an "anti-Chinese wave" in Indonesia. One week later
a CPR embassy protest used language that illustrated how
rapidly relations had deteriorated in just that short time span.
Objecting to the "brutal" search of Chinese textile specialists
by the military, the embassy charged that this constituted
"deliberate sabotage" of CPR-Indonesian relations and that
Chinese assistance would be suspended pending redress and
guarantees by the Indonesian government.

It appears, however, that Peking was prepared to step back
from an all-out anti-Indonesian campaign even in early November. NCNA, for example, reported Indonesia's official
apology for an October 16 raid on the CPR commercial coun-
selor's office but ominously added that "on the same day,
October 30, Indonesian soldiers tried to force their way into
NCNA's Djakarta office." An embassy protest on November
4 indicated that harassment of Chinese officials had spread
from Djakarta to other regional centers such as Medan where
"Medan military and governmental authorities" allegedly
"instigated" rioters in the storming of the CPR consulate
and in insulting China and Mao Tse-tung. The embassy note
claimed that the incident had "further damaged the foundation of friendly relations between China and Indonesia"
but stopped short of articulating irreparable harm.

On November 22 a new tone was sounded in the cacophony

of Chinese recriminations. Belatedly releasing the November 4 embassy protest, NCNA aired China's initial objections to "outrages" against the persons and property of Overseas Chinese by rioters who announced "that their actions had the support of the army." The protest pointed up the discrepancy between President Sukarno's appeals and the actual shift in Indonesian power by stating: "Despite President Sukarno's repeated appeals to refrain from disruptive racialist acts and to safeguard the friendly relations between China and Indonesia, all indications now point to the daily expansion rather than stoppage, of the outrageous persecution of Chinese nationals." Another embassy note, dated the nineteenth, charged armed mobs in Makassar, which "included" a number of army personnel, with assaulting Chinese nationals and destroying their property, while declaring: "We are authorized by the government to do so." Almost a month later another embassy note also claimed that mobs in Medan who attacked the Chinese consulate a second time were exhorted to do so by North Sumatran military and governmental leaders.

A further step along the road to a disruption of relations was taken in the second CPR foreign ministry protest released on February 3, 1966, which deplored "the extremely serious and barbarous attack on the embassy of the Chinese People's Republic in Indonesia by hooligans organized by Indonesian right-wing forces" perpetrated on the same day. The note insisted that the "outrage . . . was obviously planned and organized beforehand . . . with the connivance of the Indonesian government" and constituted "another grave step taken by the Indonesian right-wing forces in continuously undermining the relations between the two countries." A third foreign ministry protest, dated the twenty-seventh, covered another attack on the Makassar consulate which resulted in the "injury [of] the Chinese consul and consulate personnel." Noting that the rioters shouted "Long

live Nasution!" the foreign ministry concluded that the outrage was "obviously engineered by the right-wing forces
supporting Nasution."

Peking's inability to protect either its officials or its resident nationals, while simultaneously refusing to break diplomatic relations, seemed to accelerate the tempo of Indonesian
government-supported actions against them. A fourth foreign
ministry protest, aired on March 11, denounced "rabid attacks" on the Djakarta offices of the CPR commercial coun-
selor, the NCNA, and the consulate general during which
thirty Chinese officials were injured. The protest declared
that these outrages were "unprecedented in the history of
international relations," but it warned only weakly that "if
the Indonesian government is helpless before these most
grave incidents and fails to stop them, . . . greater damage"
would be done to bilateral relations.

With Suharto's power investiture in mid-March, the Indonesian government seemed to be encouraging Peking to
break relations. Six more official Chinese protests between
March 21 and 29 indicated how rapidly Suharto was moving
against the Chinese. A CPR foreign ministry note dated
March 27 and an "authorized" NCNA statement of March
25 protested Suharto's closure of the CPR's NCNA office in
Djakarta. The closure was depicted as an "important part"
of the Indonesian reactionaries' "wild campaign for opposing
China." While the NCNA statement declared that "the Indonesian government has now broken this link in the chain
of friendship between the Chinese and Indonesian people,"
the foreign ministry note fulminated: "the Chinese government has to warn the Indonesian government: Your unwar-
ranted action of closing down the NCNA office further dam-
ages the relations between the two countries and will have
serious consequences."

The "serious consequences" to which the note referred
seemed to mean the inauguration of a full-scale Chinese

propaganda campaign against the new Indonesian leadership, introduced by the statement that Chinese patience had finally come to an end: "until today the Chinese press has not published a single commentary on the changes in Indonesia in recent months." [29] The *People's Daily* came to the self-evident conclusion that "the Indonesian government obviously wants to worsen state relations between China and Indonesia." An embassy note on the twenty-sixth averred that because of Indonesian raids and "unreasonable restrictions," the CPR was suspending the operations of its consulates in Medan, Makassar, and Bandjarmasin—a development which could only have delighted Indonesian authorities.

Finally, still another foreign ministry note on March 26 charged the Indonesian military with "kidnapping" Chinese diplomatic personnel and detaining them at army headquarters, and still another, three days later, spotlighted a new phase of Indonesia's anti-China campaign—raids and takeovers of Overseas Chinese schools by the military-backed, anti-communist student organization, KAMI.

A spate of protests in April over further atrocities against Chinese facilities and resident Chinese was climaxed by an April 12 foreign ministry "request" that the Indonesian government arrange transportation back to China for CPR nationals who wished to return. The note clearly indicated that Peking was aware of its inability to protect its nationals in Indonesia because it could exercise no effective sanction against the Indonesian government, which was assailed in the note for "assuming the inescapable responsibility for the further worsening" of relations.

As CPR frustration grew, Indonesian student groups, with tacit government backing, continued their harassment of both official and resident Chinese, while Peking protests increased in number and severity of language. Four more protests at the foreign ministry level between April 16 and April

[29] *People's Daily* editorial, March 30, 1966.

25 angrily denounced a series of destructive raids and seizures of Chinese mission property, admitting for the first time that "the Indonesian government is pushing the relations between the two countries to the verge of a complete split." The note of April 16 concluded that by its actions it was apparent that Indonesia had now "completely sided with imperialism headed by the United States" in the "international, anti-communist, anti-Chinese chorus." The Peking press in following this up took the same tack, branding the incidents "obviously planned actions taken by the Indonesian government to disrupt completely the diplomatic relations between the two countries." [30]

Despite the anti-Chinese depredations which by the spring of 1966 had become almost a daily feature of Indonesian life, Peking did not completely break relations (and had not through December 1967, although they were "frozen" in November), primarily because of its obligation to repatriate the Overseas Chinese and because it wished to provide assurance to other Chinese communities in Southeast Asia that, despite intolerable conditions, the motherland would stand by them. Thus, in May, the Peking press laid bare the extent of Indonesia's anti-China campaign, while arguing that it did not represent the "real" feelings of the Indonesian people. Claiming that Indonesian media had featured "more than 2000 articles attacking and slandering China" and that "right-wing leaders" had "publicly maligned China as representing 'imperialism' and 'neocolonialism,' " the press rejected the Indonesian assertion that the anti-China campaign had a popular base and countered that "these outrages were by a gang of counterrevolutionary right-wingers who do not represent the Indonesian people at all. . . ." Suharto, Nasution, and Malik himself were accused of "encouraging the hooligans by their 'speeches,' 'congratulations,' and orders." And, the press concluded, "You can never escape the full criminal

[30] *People's Daily* Commentator, April 26, 1966.

responsibility for your deliberate attempt to bring about a complete break in relations between China and Indonesia" through atrocities which have "no parallels . . . in the history of international relations." [31]

The theme of Indonesia's desire to rupture relations between the two states was repeated in five embassy and foreign ministry protest notes from the time of the April 15 raid on the CPR embassy through mid-May, all of which, according to Peking, exploded the lie that Indonesia was "willing to maintain good and normal relations with China." [32]

The spring protests reflected the CPR's underlying fear that China would lose face among other Overseas Chinese, a fear which proved well-grounded when it became apparent that many Chinese in Indonesia were, for purposes of self-protection, proclaiming their loyalty to Djakarta and denouncing Peking. In order to win back lost support in the Indonesian Chinese community, Peking retreated from its initial demand that Indonesia repatriate those Chinese who wished to return to China. In still another foreign ministry note, dated May 18, it declared that because of Djakarta's refusal to perform its "incumbent duty," the Chinese government had decided to "send ships to Indonesia in the near future to receive the persecuted nationals who desire to return." The note demanded that the Indonesian authorities assure the safety of both the departing Chinese and of the ships and crews coming to meet them as well as permitting the former to retain "their own effects and funds." In addition, the note requested that "the two governments immediately hold consultations" to make "appropriate arrangements." Buttressing the foreign ministry note, Peking broadcast on the same day a statement by the Overseas Chinese Affairs Commission which emphasized that the dispatch of

[31] *People's Daily* Commentator, May 11, 1966.
[32] See, for example, the CPR embassy note carried in NCNA, May 7, 1966.

repatriation vessels indicated that the CPR did not remain "indifferent" to the plight of its nationals.

Protest meetings at Overseas Chinese farms in China (establishments in rural China where those Chinese who had lived abroad were isolated from the indigenous population) and by Overseas Chinese city groups were publicized by NCNA following the new declaration that ships would be sent. These meetings condemned Indonesian authorities and graphically recounted the atrocities perpetrated on the Chinese in Indonesia by the "right-wing military clique." As for those Chinese who pledged allegiance to the Suharto government, they were conveniently branded "agents of the Chaing Kai-shek gang." [33]

Anticipating its limited ability to assist its nationals in the near future, despite the promise to send ships, Peking propaganda encouraged the Overseas Chinese to remain steadfast and to resist "cowardly" attacks. As one returned Chinese put it: "With the powerful socialist motherland behind us and the great leader Chairman Mao as our guide, we Chinese nationals are not to be bullied."

Another theme developed at Overseas Chinese meetings on the mainland consisted of separating "the masses of the Indonesian people" who desire to live in friendship with their Chinese neighbors from the "handful of Indonesian reactionaries." The purpose of this campaign was to obfuscate the fact of widespread, popular anti-Chinese feeling in Indonesia, depicting it instead as a series of isolated incidents which had occurred only because the Indonesian government had fomented them. NCNA, for example, stated: "Many Chinese nationals now returned from Indonesia recalled how their Indonesian friends had condemned the small handful of right-wing forces as the scum of the Indo-

[33] Peking Radio in Indonesian, May 12 and 13, 1966; NCNA, July 16, 1966; and Chinese embassy note, July 26, 1966.

nesian nation who had crushed the Indonesian people's aspirations by destroying the traditional friendship between the
people of China and Indonesia." [34]

The Chinese press carried the same interpretation of an
isolated Indonesian leadership and the "great heroism" displayed by the Overseas Chinese. It stated categorically: "Under whatever circumstances the Chinese government has the
responsibility for protecting the legitimate rights and interests of its nationals abroad." [35] Yet it was precisely this responsibility for the Overseas Chinese that Peking seemed
unable to fulfill despite its endless official fulminations—six
in the month of June alone. A foreign ministry note on June
29 exasperatedly observed that the Indonesian government
had not even deigned to reply to the CPR note of May 18,
offering repatriation ships and asking for immediate negotiations. Moreover, "the Indonesian Government had resorted
to frantic lies, slander, and intimidation, alleging that there
was ammunition on the Chinese ships sent to Indonesia and
threatening that anyone who wanted to leave would be sent
to Taiwan. . . ." A subsequent NCNA report rejected an
alleged Indonesian demand that all who wished to return to
China provide their names to regional officials as a device
"to step up the persecution of the Overseas Chinese on the
list." [36] Meanwhile, NCNA urged the Overseas Chinese to
keep faith: ". . . thanks to the backing of the powerful socialist motherland, the time has gone when the Overseas
Chinese were at the mercy of others."

In early September the Indonesian government agreed to
the dispatch of Chinese vessels, in all likelihood to relieve
the pressure on the regional camps which had been set up
for displaced Chinese in the aftermath of the coup. Subsequent Chinese protests, however, charged that the camps
were used by Indonesian authorities for the harassment and

[34] NCNA, May 20, 1966.
[35] *Ta Kung Pao* editorial, May 22, 1966.
[36] NCNA, July 5, 1966.

wholesale robbery of its Chinese inhabitants who were treated more as criminals than emigrants. In mid-September Djakarta launched a regular anti-Chinese radio program which undoubtedly had the effect of fanning the flames of racial hatred still further. The initial broadcast, for example, declared that "Chinese citizens of the CPR are making a fortune and taking it easy in Indonesia, . . . conducting activities designed to prevent the improvement of the Indonesian people's economy so that the living conditions of the Indonesian people would worsen." [37]

As Chinese protests grew in frequency and intensity following what Peking termed Djakarta's unreasonable rejection "of its demands for facilitating the repatriation of its nationals," Indonesian media responded by increasing their own allegations against the resident Chinese to justify the anti-Chinese actions which were occurring and seemingly to encourage more: "The Chinese nationals in general have shown an attitude and view not in accord with the aspirations of the Indonesian nation. . . . On top of that, many of them were clearly involved in the counterrevolutionary Gestapu/PKI movement, as a result of which the local people of the regions expressed strong resentment against a continuing stay of those Chinese nationals in their midst." [38] The Chinese responded with the charge that "all indications show that the Indonesian right-wing reactionary forces are plotting to whip up a new anti-China and anti-Chinese high tide on a scale greater than ever before. . . ." [39] In an account of the first repatriation ship to return with a full complement of Chinese, Peking again acknowledged its lack of effective leverage on Djakarta, declaring: "The victimized Chinese nationals point out that it is impossible for the Indonesian authorities to deny their cruel persecution of Chi-

[37] Djakarta Domestic Service, September 15, 1966.
[38] ANTARA, September 27, 1966.
[39] CPR embassy note, September 30, 1966, carried in NCNA, October 4, 1966; and NCNA commentary, October 4, 1966.

nese nationals. The Indonesian authorities will certainly be severely condemned by right-minded public opinion the world over." [40]

Even more ominously, Peking reported that regional authorities in Indonesia were openly passing anti-Chinese resolutions to rob them of their livelihood and to require them to register "in preparation for a large-scale anti-Chinese campaign." [41] The only alternative available to many Chinese was a declaration of allegiance to Indonesia and a renunciation of the CPR. Returning Overseas Chinese alleged that Chiang Kai-shek agents of the Indonesian government tried to dissuade them but were sometimes rebuffed.

> If you go back you will have to eat grit and grass roots, and you'll have nothing to look forward to but death. But if you join the "Allegiance Society" (a reactionary organization of the Chiang Kai-shek group) your whole family can stay here. . . . The young man immediately got hold of the Chiang Kai-shek man and told him sternly: "You want me to turn against my motherland. I'll never do that! I love my motherland and will never become so degraded as to turn traitor." [42]

Peking was faced with a delicate problem as a result of the repatriation of several thousand Indonesian Chinese, most of whom had lived there for generations and had never seen their homeland, much less been subjected to the rigors of a communist system. The solution was twofold: isolation from the rest of society to diminish the possible adverse bourgeois influence on Chinese life; and resocialization of the repatriated to the norms of that society. The problem was particularly complex because most of the Chinese in Indonesia were not peasant farmers but entrepreneurs, traders, and shopkeepers. In short, they possessed attitudes and skills which

[40] NCNA October 4, 1966.
[41] Ibid., October 6, 1966.
[42] Ibid., October 20, 1966.

could not be readily utilized by a CPR in the midst of the "Great Cultural Revolution."

Chinese media indicated that the resocialization process began almost immediately upon disembarkation, when Red Guards met the repatriates in Chankiang and the latter "pledged their determination to learn from the Red Guards, to study Chairman Mao's works diligently, and to take an active part in China's socialist revolution and construction." [43] At a reception the following day, a representative of the returned Chinese declared that "side by side with the people throughout the country, they would take up the hoe in one hand and rifle in the other, share in militia training and defend the socialist motherhood. . . . We will go anywhere the motherland requires. We will use our hands to contribute to the socialist motherland." [44] Stories were featured in which returned Chinese "clasped the hands of the Red Guards and said: 'I will do my best to learn from you so that one day I, too, can become a Red Guard of Chairman Mao.'" [45] It is noteworthy, however, that most of the Chinese discussed in the media were apparently young, indicating that Peking had probably decided to focus its resocialization efforts on that segment of the returnees who would be most susceptible to change. As for those Chinese who remained in Indonesia, the following advice was tendered: "The patriotic Overseas Chinese have not reconciled themselves to being pushed around at the whim of the Indonesian reactionary forces. There is oppression and there is resistance. To survive one must carry out struggle . . . inspired by the invincible thought of Mao Tse-tung and fearless of violence and even of being beheaded, become united and persist in struggle, and finally return to our motherland in triumph." [46]

[43] *Ibid.*, October 10, 1966.
[44] *Ibid.*, October 11, 1966.
[45] *Ibid.*, October 12, 1966.
[46] *Ibid.*, October 16, 1966.

Mutual hostility spiraled even as repatriation proceeded, as each side increased its propaganda charges against the other. In late October, the CPR protested what it termed a "serious stage" in the Indonesian anti-Chinese campaign— "expelling Chinese nationals en masse" from a number of provinces. Peking insisted that "the dispatch of ships by the Chinese government to bring back its persecuted nationals does not in the least mean that the Indonesian government can shirk its duty toward the persecuted Chinese nationals. Still less does it mean that the Indonesian government can expel Chinese nationals at will." [47] Less than one month later, denouncing "ceaseless atrocious persecution of innocent Chinese residents," ranging from attacks, sabotage, blackmail, and plunder to beating, insults, and murder, the CPR embassy pleaded: "According to the treaty and agreement signed by the Chinese and Indonesian governments on the question of overseas nationals, the Indonesian government bears an inescapable responsibility for the protection of the lawful rights and interests of Chinese residents in Indonesia." [48] In an attempt to depict these Indonesian actions as unpopular, Peking once again claimed that "many Indonesians defied the danger to their lives to visit the homes of persecuted Chinese, express sympathy and bring them food." Indonesian peasants reportedly told their Chinese friends: "We regard your fate as our own. We shall overthrow the reactionaries one day, revenge you, and settle accounts with them." [49]

Peking noted that anti-Chinese "decrees" which had lain dormant since the 1950's were being reinstated, prohibiting Overseas Chinese from operating retail businesses, and that Nasution had outlined a master-plan for dealing with CPR nationals which called for "a large-scale massacre, deportation

[47] CPR Foreign Ministry Note, October 21, 1966.
[48] CPR Embassy Note, November 15, 1966.
[49] NCNA, December 4, 1966, and February 13, 1967.

en masse, and an assimilation project." [50] Indulging their
penchant for models by which to maintain the spirits of the
remaining Chinese in Indonesia and to inspire the home
front to greater deeds of adulation of Chairman Mao, Chinese media inaugurated a publicity campaign for forty-one
young Overseas Chinese who had allegedly been incarcerated
and abused before being returned. Chen I spoke at a Peking
rally in their honor, with both home and foreign audiences
undoubtedly in mind:

> Their struggle and subsequent victory have utterly destroyed
> the reactionary arrogance of the Indonesian fascists and the
> imperialists, and have given a tremendous lift to the revolu-
> tionary morale of the patriotic Chinese nationals abroad. . . .
> We solemnly call to the attention of the Indonesian govern-
> ment the fact that the Chinese people, armed with the thought
> of Mao Tse-tung, are not to be bullied, and no persecution of
> the nationals abroad of mighty socialist China will be toler-
> ated.[51]

As Indonesian regional authorities continued their systematic destruction of the Chinese economic position within
the country, even East Java, the last stronghold of pro-Su-
karno/pro-PKI sentiment, succumbed. According to the CPR
embassy, the regional commander Sumitro announced that
"shops run by Chinese nationals, including even their stocks
and equipment" would be confiscated by February 1967.
Thrown back to the realization that the CPR had no chance
of obstructing these plans, Chinese officials turned to the
same arguments which other status quo powers had used
against China when it was on the offensive—an appeal to
international law: "Where else on earth is there a government like yours which brazenly tramples on the guiding principles of international relations and on the treaties and agreements concluded between two countries and which en-

[50] *Ibid.*, December 6, 1966.
[51] *Ibid.*, December 29, 1966.

croaches to such an appalling and flagrant extent on the proper rights and interests of the nationals of a country with which it has diplomatic relations?" [52]

Perhaps encouraged by Peking's propaganda attestations of support, but more likely simply concerned with maintaining their livelihood, Chinese in East Java resisted the Indonesian decrees. This course of action led to direct confrontations between demonstrating Chinese and the military, and in April it resulted in the death and injury of a number of Chinese. The CPR embassy complained: "Obviously, the bloody incident was premeditated and carefully planned by the Indonesian Government." The note went on predictably to exhort "the broad masses of Chinese nationals who are armed with Mao Tse-tung's thought"—"never yield to oppression or be cowed." [53] By this time, however, such bravado seemed designed more to inspire those at home than to ease the plight of the Chinese in Indonesia who, if anything, had perceived Peking's attentions as counterproductive, since each protest seemed to be followed by more intense persecution. Indeed, an Overseas Chinese Affairs Commission statement tacitly acknowledged this state of affairs in protesting Indonesian depredations and then concluded: "We believe that you will hold still higher the great red banner of Mao Tse-tung's thought and will wage an unremitting struggle to defend your own just rights." [54]

By the end of April relations had sunk to their lowest level without actually rupturing. At that time the embassies of both states were being besieged in their respective host capitals. In dismissing two Chinese diplomats, Foreign Minister Malik placed the blame for anti-Chinese demonstrations in Indonesia squarely on the CPR: "The evidence in the hands

[52] CPR Embassy Note, January 17, 1967, released by NCNA, January 30, 1967. For a description of parallel problems in Sino-Indonesian relations in 1959–60, see Hinton, *China in World Politics,* pp. 431–33.

[53] CPR Embassy notes, April 8 and 12, 1967; ANTARA, April 12, 1967.

[54] NCNA, April 23, 1967.

of the government indicates that the CPR embassy and consulate general have masterminded the incidents in Djakarta and the regions and thereby have caused a further worsening of relations between Indonesia and the CPR." [55] For its part, Peking issued a statement summarizing Indonesian atrocities since the coup attempt of October 1965 and claiming that the "right-wing military clique headed by Suharto and Nasution" had "attacked and raided Chinese diplomatic missions more than 30 times, wounded more than 40 Chinese diplomatic and consular personnel and correspondents, . . . forcibly occupied more than 10 office and residential premises, . . . and perpetrated a series of outrages which have rarely been seen in the history of international relations." As for the Overseas Chinese, they were urged to sustain the good fight, for: "We are firmly convinced that a new revolutionary high tide is bound to arrive in Indonesia." [56]

Despite popular pressure for the severance of diplomatic relations, including an Indonesian Cooperation Parliament resolution on June 16, Malik resisted. He insisted that such action should only be taken as a "last resort and that the government would try to force the CPR government to repatriate its citizens from Indonesia," a statement which was probably correctly interpreted by Peking as meaning "more rabid suppression and persecution of the Chinese Nationals." [57] Both sides apparently calculated that a formal break in relations would not further the policies of either. Peking seemed to prefer retaining a formal presence to provide at least a modicum of assistance to its nationals, making formal arrangements for repatriation, and serving as a listening post for any further outrages with which its propaganda machine could be fueled. Furthermore, in time, the CPR diplomatic establishment might be able to supply a resurgent Peking-

[55] Djakarta Domestic Service, April 24, 1967.
[56] CPR Government Statement, April 26, 1967.
[57] Djakarta Domestic Service, June 16, 1967; NCNA, June 21, 1967.

based PKI. On Djakarta's part, a diplomatic post in Peking provided the government with intelligence concerning its new enemy's policies as well as an opportunity to observe the activities of the large number of expatriate Indonesians who chose to remain in China for political reasons rather than face the prospect of a military tribunal by returning home. Nevertheless, Indonesian leaders seized every opportunity they could to embarrass the CPR and to expose its ineffectiveness, even going to the extent of *officially* adopting the insulting expression *"Tjina"* to replace *"Tionghoa"* when referring to the Chinese. A rough English equivalent of the former would be "Chink!" [58]

PEKING'S SEVERANCE OF ECONOMIC TIES AND INTERNATIONAL POLITICAL COOPERATION

There is some evidence to support the contention that the CPR did not view the new Indonesian situation as entirely antithetical until Suharto's power investiture in March 1966. Thus, as late as December 9, 1965, Peking decided to fulfill a shipping agreement made with Indonesia prior to the coup. According to the Chinese account, the first Chinese freighter to call at Indonesia under the agreement had an official delegation on board. Its leader declared that "nobody could undermine the militant friendship between the Chinese and the Indonesian people." [59] Djakarta media apparently ignored the Chinese ship and implied instead that Peking was attempting to exert at least indirect economic pressure on Indonesia by ordering its aid experts to leave their projects in mid-December, and by ending rubber purchases from Indonesia and turning instead to "Nekolim" Singapore. Peking media began to disseminate stories of Indonesia's economic

[58] Djakarta Domestic Service, July 25, 1967.
[59] NCNA, December 9, 1965. Note the significant omission of any reference to the Indonesian government, however.

plight, a situation which was never acknowledged during the "alliance" period. Finally, in April 1966, after continued harassment of its officials, Peking decided to withdraw its remaining aid personnel because current Indonesian actions had "destroyed the basis of economic cooperation between the two countries." [60] In other words, Peking was cutting the last cooperative bond between the two states because it could no longer serve as a source of influence. Chinese aid personnel, many of whom had undoubtedly doubled as political agents for the CPR, had become potential hostages of a hostile regime instead. Peking had no choice but to recall them.

The severance of economic links was a relatively uncomplicated task compared with the conflict that occurred between the two states with respect to representation in Afro-Asian councils and radical front organizations of the international communist movement. Whereas economic ties could be unilaterally cut, Peking's attempt to displace the new anti-communist Indonesian regime from its predecessor's positions in international radical groups was bound to erupt in conflict and in attempts to form opposing coalitions.

The first manifestation of this conflict appeared at the end of December 1965. At that time Peking media carried an appeal from the pro-Chinese, Djakarta-based Afro-Asian Journalists Association (AAJA) to its CPR affiliate protesting "harassment" and "arbitrary interference in the affairs of the AAJA" by the Indonesian armed forces and by the recently reorganized Indonesian Journalists Association which was now engaged in purging its former PKI membership.[61] In a separate item on the same day, NCNA reported that the AAJA had decided "to withdraw the secretariat temporarily from Djakarta" after a "thorough study of the situation in

---

[60] CPR foreign ministry note, April 18, 1966.
[61] NCNA, December 30, 1965.

Indonesia since last October." In fact the secretariat was relocated in Peking in January 1967, and from there it has been sniping at the Indonesian government ever since.

Perhaps the most interesting imbroglio created by Sino-Indonesian competition within international front groups occurred at the January 1966 Tricontinental Conference in Havana. Two Indonesian delegations arrived, one officially sponsored by the new Indonesian government, which undoubtedly wished to present a bill-of-particulars concerning Peking's interference in Indonesian affairs, and the other composed of Indonesia's long-time, pro-Peking representative at the AAPSO secretariat in Cairo, Ibrahim Isa, along with some leftist Indonesian journalists who had remained in Peking where they had been visiting at the time of the coup. When the Isa group was recognized, the Indonesian government recalled its official delegation and withdrew the passports of all members of the rump delegation, a rather ineffective sanction since all of them were now resident in Peking! Although the U.S.S.R., Mongolia, and Nepal opposed Ibrahim Isa's resolution to place the Indonesian situation on the agenda, it was nonetheless discussed.

Making no reference to the difficulty over delegations, Peking reported Isa's address to the conference in which he excoriated Indonesian trends led by the military "in close cooperation with and under the instigation of international imperialism headed by the United States' CIA." [62] NCNA also reported that Isa had announced in Havana the "formation of a new leadership of the Indonesian organization for Afro-Asian solidarity" since "over half" the Indonesian solidarity organization's plenum had been arrested. Isa promised to continue operations from abroad (Peking) since "there could be no possibility at all for the organization to function properly in Indonesia." [63]

[62] *Ibid.*, January 8, 1966.
[63] *Ibid.*, January 15, 1966.

Peking has employed such Peking-based front groups as the AAJA and the Isa organization-in-exile to provide an aura of international support for its anti-Indonesian campaign, just as it earlier had used these organizations against the Soviet Union. In April 1966, for example, the AAJA's fourth plenum, which was convened in Peking, predictably denounced Indonesian events. The head of the AAJA, Djawoto, who had just resigned as Indonesian ambassador to China, denounced the Indonesian government as reactionary and anti-Chinese and berated the Indonesian Journalists Association for purging its pro-China members, launching an anti-China campaign, and selling out to U.S. imperialism. Injecting the Sino-Soviet dispute into the meeting, the so-called Indonesian delegate to the plenum, Supeno, charged that "sham revolutionaries had played a shameless role in current Indonesian events. While pretending to support the Indonesian progressives, they had actually inspired the Indonesian rightists to launch the campaign of terror." Branding them "apologists" for imperialism, Supeno concluded: "We can never unite with those who consider the common enemy of the world's people, U.S. imperialism, as a friend, and who consider a comrade-in-arms like the great Chinese people their chief enemy." [64]

By mid-1967, Peking was using the AAJA as still another sounding board for international publicity for the Great Cultural Revolution (GCR). Djawoto enthused that "the AAJA had become stronger and more militant since its secretariat had moved to Peking" and urged that it should now "organize the Afro-Asian journalists to study, apply, and propagate Mao Tse-tung's thought, . . . and China's Great Cultural Revolution." [65] Concluding the fifth plenary meeting, Djawoto noted: "Our secretariat meeting has adopted Chairman Mao Tse-tung's thoughts as the new line of policy in

[64] *Ibid.*, April 24, 1966.
[65] *Ibid.*, June 15, 1967.

every field of our activities. . . . Chairman Mao's thought contains universal truth applicable to all stages of revolutionary struggle in every country the world over." [66] Thus, as the CPR's foreign policy requirements changed during the course of the GCR the Maoists in the foreign ministry employed their tools for new purposes. Whereas the AAJA was initially used after the coup to discredit the new Indonesian government, its task had shifted in 1967 to that of adding to the contrived international adulation for Chairman Mao as the GCR forced Peking to turn inward away from foreign affairs and focus on its own domestic power struggle.

[66] *Ibid.*, June 17, 1967.

❂ 7

Peking's Reaction to the Destruction of the PKI

One of the most important conveyors of Chinese influence in Indonesia prior to the coup was the PKI whose intimate relationship with the Indonesian government has been described in the first part of this study. The table in the preceding chapter (and the subsequent discussion) indicated that Peking's most persistent concern in the post-coup period was Indonesia's treatment of CPR officials and the Overseas Chinese community—both groups for which the CPR assumed direct responsibility. Considerably less attention was devoted to the fate of the PKI: only 42 theme/commentaries (14 per cent) out of a total of 308 devoted to Indonesia from October 1965 through December 1967. It is this comparatively slight concern with the fate and future of Peking's party ally that I propose to examine in this chapter, suggesting a priori that the small quantity of Peking's attention (though not its substance) might be explained by a Chinese desire to underplay the devastation to the PKI's organization and the decimation of its leadership.

An additional explanation for minimal Chinese attention may be found in Lin Piao's September 1965 tract on "people's war," in which he stressed self-reliance for indigenous com-

munist parties, apparently in situations of either success or
failure. Moreover, the accumulation of much circumstantial
evidence which pointed to a Chinese role in the coup attempt
probably motivated Chinese decision-makers to remain relatively silent in hopes of avoiding further exposure and
embarrassing denunciation to both itself and the PKI.

The time lag between the destruction of the party and
the first public indications from Peking that a new party
was being formed (April–June 1966) may have been the
result of internal conflicts within the CCP (related to the
power and ideological disputes of the Great Cultural Revolution) over the causes of the PKI defeat and what new
course of action a renovated party should pursue. As we
shall see, the PKI question had become intimately involved
in GCR politics, particularly since Liu Shao-chi and Peng
Chen were both associated with Peking's previous coalition
policy vis-à-vis Djakarta and at least acquiesced to the PKI's
plan peacefully to subvert the Indonesian power balance.

Interestingly, the PKI leadership seemed ambivalent about
its policy of peaceful power accretion, particularly as the
party acquired a mass base in the 1960's, thereby sacrificing
ideological orthodoxy to strength of numbers. Aidit had
warned against the potentially unreliable nature of these
new members over a year before the coup occurred:

> All of these classes both when they are struggling against the
> proletariat as well as when they are cooperating with the
> proletariat, constantly use unstable elements within the party
> to enter the head and heart of the party . . . and continuously
> influence the ideology . . . and actions of the party and pro-
> letariat.
>
> Thus, it is clear that the source of the petit bourgeois
> ideology which emerges in the party is the ocean of petit bour-
> geois around the members of the party, the majority of whom
> come from this class.[1]

[1] *Harian Rakjat,* August 10, 1964, in JPRS, *Translations on South and East
Asia,* 61 (September 10, 1964): 7–8.

It was the petit bourgeois membership, on whose support both the PKI and CCP had counted, which proved so ephemeral in the coup aftermath and which even acted in the succeeding months as a fifth column to locate and destroy other party members. Peking's reactions to these developments paralleled its response to the depredations committed against its own nationals, though on a smaller scale and a lower level of authoritativeness. In short, Peking realized that its ability to save the PKI was even less than its ability to protect the Overseas Chinese community.

REFUSAL TO ACKNOWLEDGE AIDIT'S DEATH

One of the first indicators of the CPR's desire to underplay the extent of the PKI's destruction at the hands of the Indonesian military was Peking's treatment of Aidit's fate. Refusing to acknowledge either his flight or his death, Chinese media cited international sources to create the impression that Aidit was still leading the party. The head of the New Zealand Communist Party (pro-Peking), Wilcox, was quoted as stating that only one force could defeat the Indonesian military "and that is the PKI led by D. N. Aidit." [2] In its roundup of Western comment on the coup, the *People's Daily* included a French report that "Aidit is leading the communists to wage armed struggle" in the mountains of Central Java. A less sanguine possibility was also cited, however, from the *Christian Science Monitor,* which noted that the PKI's "roots go deep underground" and that the party is well equipped for "clandestine survival, whatever happens to its leaders." [3] The Chinese continued to publish messages through the remainder of 1965 intimating that Aidit was still leading the PKI. [4]

[2] NCNA, November 4, 1965.
[3] *People's Daily,* November 7, 1965.
[4] See, for example, the Australian Communist Party (pro-Peking) message to Aidit carried by NCNA, November 18, 1965, and the Burmese Communist Party statement carried by NCNA, January 6, 1966.

Peking did not refer to the PKI on its own authority until early December, however, and only then to excoriate "Indonesian right-wing papers" for spreading "preposterous rumors" concerning Aidit's "whereabouts" with the "obvious aim of worsening the relations between China and Indonesia." The Chinese report dismissed the "barefaced lie" that Aidit and PKI Deputy Chairman Njoto had fled Indonesia in a "submarine belonging to a foreign country," deploring this "rumor" as an attack on China "by insinuation." The report went on to refute rumors that Aidit had been killed. In a clear endorsement of Aidit's leadership, Peking portrayed the "rumor-mongering" as a device to create confusion about "Chairman Aidit because he is the outstanding helmsman of the PKI, . . . fights resolutely against U.S.-led imperialism, colonialism, and neocolonialism as well as against modern revisionism and modern dogmatism, . . . and enjoys high prestige both at home and abroad." [5]

Nonetheless, by the end of the year, Chinese officials may have concluded that the pretense was becoming transparent. In an interview with the Japanese newspaper *Mainichi,* the head of the China-Japan Trade Office, Liao Ching-chih, was reported to have said: "I cannot say anything for sure about the report of Chairman Aidit's death," after which he noted cryptically that during the course of China's revolution, Mao Tse-tung had also been reported slain "a number of times." [6] Peking's last effort (known to this author) to hide Aidit's death occurred in February 1966 when Chinese media in summarizing a Japan Communist Party statement on the Indonesian situation, excised references to accounts of Aidit's demise. [7]

Peking proved more ingenuous in its disclosure of the general crackdown on the PKI by the military throughout

[5] NCNA, December 2, 1965, and *People's Daily,* December 3, 1965.

[6] *Mainichi,* December 25, 1965.

[7] NCNA, February 8, 1966.

Indonesia. In a lengthy December account, Chinese media reported the dissolution of party branches by military decree in Djakarta, Sumatra, Sulawesi, West Java, and Kalimantan.[8] Earlier, Peking had reported that the military-controlled Supreme Operations Command had decided to try those involved in the coup attempt before "a special military tribunal," a decision which Peking stated was made at a meeting "presided over by President Sukarno." [9] Peking also publicized Nasution's vow to "crush" the PKI and "purge their people from state organs, military agencies, and other revolutionary organizations." [10] Peking portrayed Sukarno as approving Nasution's crackdown by disseminating Nasution's remark that "Bung Karno . . . has reminded us that the PKI uses guerrilla tactics in the political field[,] . . . therefore, guerrilla tactics should also be unfolded in the political field in our purge movement." [11]

INDONESIAN ATTEMPTS TO LINK THE CPR TO THE PKI COUP

Peking had good cause to fear the creation of a public tribunal to expose the *Gestapu* affair. Under military control such a series of trials could be manipulated to discredit completely the PKI and Sukarno and to link China with the coup attempt. Peking's apprehensions proved well-founded as the trials of PKI members, leftist military, and high level "old order" officials were conducted during 1966 and 1967. With representatives of the Suharto government serving as both prosecutors and judges, the results of the "trials" could easily be predicted. Their political function was to serve as well-publicized negative examples for future Indonesian political aspirants (borrowing a technique from the CPR) and to lay bare the incredible corruption of the Sukarno

[8] *Ibid.,* December 7, 1965.
[9] *Ibid.,* December 3, 1965.
[10] *Ibid.,* December 10, 1965.
[11] *Ibid.,* December 24, 1965.

era. In pursuing the latter end, Suharto cast himself in much the same role Ne Win did in Burma after seizing power from U Nu's Anti-Fascist People's Freedom League. The difference between the two lay in the actions they followed after discrediting their respective old orders: Ne Win chose to isolate Burma while Suharto opted for the re-establishment of Western economic links and Indonesian aspirations to regional leadership.

The September 1966 trial of Jusuf Muda Dalam, former Central Banking Affairs Minister, is a good example of the Indonesian government's strategy. Dalam was accused of mismanaging over $270 million. During the course of his defense, he managed to implicate Sukarno by claiming that all of his acts were approved by the president and that he "was only responsible to the president." [12] The prosecution, in addition, wished to link Dalam to both Sukarno and the PKI: "The prosecutor emphatically stated that the accused, when viewed from all his actions and the resultant harmful effects on the national economy and misery of the Indonesian people, could be said to be as a minister, having the morality of a degenerate of the old order . . . , and hence the accused could easily have been used by the PKI." [13]

Nasution had actually laid the groundwork for implicating Peking within two months of the coup. In December 1965, Chinese media complained that he was attacking the CPR "by innuendo and by name" in order to link it with Gestapu.[14] The Indonesian press agency ANTARA in the last week of December carried reports that in the aftermath of the coup the PKI "had been ordered to stand by to receive arms from People's China." Aidit's alleged confession published in February 1966 in the Japanese press did not help the CPR's claim of innocence. Aidit attributed the coup's

[12] *Duta Masjarakat,* September 9, 1966, in JPRS, *Translations on South and East Asia,* 134 (October 18, 1966): 24.
[13] *Duta Masjarakat,* September 6, 1966, in *ibid.,* pp. 19–20.
[14] NCNA, December 10, 1965.

failure to its prematurity and to Peking's inability to assist. He further implicated China in pre-coup plotting by mentioning his stopover in Peking in August for talks "with the CCP leaders on President Sukarno's health and other matters." [15]

The Chinese chose an Albanian source to publicize their first editorial reaction to the convocation of "Mahmilub," citing a *Zeri I Popullit* article which excoriated Indonesian military preparations "for a trial of the Indonesian communists and other patriots by a special military court . . . a premeditated criminal plot . . . instigated by U.S. imperialism." [16] As for the future of the PKI, Peking displayed concern over the prospects of the CPSU coming in to pick up the pieces. Quoting the pro-Peking *Malayan Monitor,* the Chinese reported its charge that "renegades from the PKI" are trying to organize a "pseudo-communist party" with the aid of the CPSU which has "vilified as adventurists and sectarianists the PKI . . . under the chairmanship of comrade D. N. Aidit." [17]

While Peking chose to react to the military tribunal by publicizing proxy condemnations, North Vietnam actually "founded a 10-member committee of lawyers and designated several lawyers to defend the persecuted Indonesian patriots and democrats." They went so far as to submit briefs "to President Sukarno with a view to defending Njono and Lieutenant Colonel Untung, illegally sentenced to death by the Djakarta Special Military Council." [18]

Concurrent with the "Mahmilub" sessions, Indonesian leaders sought to reinforce the trials' impact by analyzing the negative effects of the old order's triangular alliance consisting of the PKI-CPR-Sukarno. Thus, Foreign Minister Malik ascribed Indonesia's deteriorated relations with India

[15] *Asahi*, February 7, 1966.
[16] NCNA, February 8, 1966.
[17] *Ibid.*, March 2, 1966.
[18] VNA, July 2, 1966.

to CPR-PKI pressure: "As a result of the CPR's interference via the PKI, there was a slogan in Indonesia: 'A victory for the CPR is a victory for Indonesia. A defeat for the CPR is a defeat for Indonesia.' " [19] Malik also pointed out that the CPR wanted Indonesia to sever not only its ties with the West but also those with the Soviet Union: "Thus, Marshal Chen I's remarks about the achievements of a policy of self-reliance by the CPR and Indonesia were meant to persuade Djakarta to reject aid from the West as well as from the Soviet Union." [20]

Djakarta media, in their account of Subandrio's trial in October 1966, also dwelt on his admission that the PKI worked as a "pressure group" for "the CPR to prevent the government from establishing good relations with the Soviet Union and Yugoslavia" and that the PKI plan to create a fifth force of armed workers and peasants "was reached after CPR Premier Chou En-lai had promised to supply light arms to equip volunteers in the framework of the Crush Malaysia Campaign." [21] Subandrio himself intimated that his use of the forged Gilchrist document, which suggested a plot by the United States, Great Britain, and the Indonesian military to overthrow Sukarno, was for the purpose of committing the CPR to a defense arrangement which "would convince England that an attack on Indonesia would not just lead to a local war, and would prove that Indonesia was not isolated." [22]

The subsequent trial of Air Force Commander Omar Dhani added to the web of charges against the CPR, particularly since Dhani's mission to Peking two weeks before the coup was taken without General Nasution's knowledge, nor,

[19] Djakarta Domestic Service, September 23, 1966.

[20] *Ibid.*

[21] Djakarta Domestic Service, October 3, 1966; and *Duta Masjarakat,* October 4, 1966, in JPRS, *Translations on South and East Asia,* 139 (December 27, 1966): 4–5.

[22] *Duta Masjarakat,* October 18, 1966, in *ibid.,* p. 26.

Nasution testified, had the Air Force ever requisitioned light weapons through him.[23] According to Dhani, whatever had been done by the Air Force with respect to training the fifth force "was based on President Sukarno's orders." [24]

Moscow, although voicing its objections to the PKI debacle, was nonetheless gleeful over Peking's implication in the coup plot as revealed in the Subandrio and Dhani trials. Using the PKI case to further its position in the polemic, Moscow held that the "Indonesian tragedy" was the consequence of Chinese "adventurism." Under Mao, "Chinese domestic and foreign policy and attempts to interfere in other countries' affairs are undermining the faith of the emerging countries which previously were sympathetic toward the CPR." [25] Continuing in the same vein, a January 1967 issue of the Soviet weekly *New Times* admitted that "some PKI leaders" supported the coup because "Peking exerted much influence upon PKI leadership, attempting to enforce an adventurous course on them. . . ." [26] Finally, in a recapitulation of the errors of Indonesian foreign policy during the Sukarno regime, Radio Moscow pinpointed President Sukarno's mistake: the creation "of the so-called Djakarta-Peking axis" which suited "the Peking dogmatists, who seek to play the national liberation movement off against other revolutionary forces. This resulted in Indonesia's partial departure from the progressive forces of the present and its isolation." Somewhat hypocritically, Radio Moscow adopted a holier-than-thou attitude toward confrontation (which it had also supported, though less enthusiastically than Peking) by claiming: "The pressure brought to bear by the Chinese adventurists was responsible also for the dangerous policy of confrontation with Malaysia." [27]

[23] Djakarta Domestic Service, December 10, 1966.
[24] *Ibid.,* December 20, 1966.
[25] Moscow Radio Peace and Progress, December 27, 1966.
[26] Summarized in *Tass,* January 18, 1967.
[27] Moscow Domestic Service, March 16, 1967.

When Sukarno attempted to lay part of the blame for Gestapu on Nasution in his "Nawaksara" speech of January 10, 1967, the latter saw his opening for a full-scale assault on Sukarno's coddling of the PKI since 1960, including his countermanding of military plans to suppress the party that year. Nasution charged that Sukarno, on PKI orders, had circumscribed the general's powers beginning in 1964, and that at the time of the coup itself he "did not contact the army . . . but, in fact, contacted the Air Force. . . . The president felt safe with the Gestapu at Halem and not with Kostrad" (the army command which ultimately put down the coup). And if this were not enough, Nasution added, Sukarno tried to implement Aidit's solution to the coup by insisting that all forces work together again as though nothing had happened, and by demanding that the military return its powers to the police and the PKI-dominated national front. Finally, Nasution concluded, a military investigation of Gestapu had demonstrated without a doubt "Sukarno's advanced knowledge of and involvement in the Gestapu incident." [28]

By 1967 Sukarno had been effectively eliminated as an actor in Indonesian politics, and the military regime and its mass media outlets were able to concentrate on connecting the CPR and Overseas Chinese to Gestapu. Thus, in late March, in Djakarta, an alleged CPR spy was apprehended who had distributed literature which "called on Chinese aliens here to launch opposition against the government led by Acting President General Suharto." A report on the arrest noted that "initial investigations show that the movement was organized from outside the country." [29] Depredations against Overseas Chinese were actually encouraged by the press. The paper *Bintang Indonesia*, for example, declared

---

[28] For a summary of Nasution's speech, see Djakarta Domestic Service, February 13, 1967.

[29] ANTARA, April 1, 1967.

that the earnings of Chinese merchants were "helping People's China to expand its economic operations" and that "most likely the proceeds from sales of the Chinese goods were utilized for the financing of subversive actions, notably to help the comeback of the PKI." [30]

By late April, the Greater Djakarta military commander, Major General Amir Machmud, called for the displacement of Chinese merchants: "We all know that the role of Chinese aliens in Indonesia is still dominant in the economic field. Therefore, we must be able within a short period to take over their role, especially in the field of distribution. . . . The greater part of the 115,000 aliens here [in Djakarta] are from People's China . . . who are undoubtedly closely associated with the Gestapu-PKI." [31] Responding to remarks like Machmud's, Peking noted apprehensively that "the Chiang Kai-shek gang will soon send a mission to Djakarta to help differentiate between Chinese communists and Taiwan Chinese." [32]

To complete Indonesia's bill-of-particulars against the CPR, Foreign Minister Malik stated in a press conference that China was training "some 100 Indonesian adventurers" in Wuhan. This provided proof, he maintained, that "the Gestapu-PKI event resulted from CPR pressure on the Gestapu-PKI group to start a rebellion for the purpose of lessening pressure on itself arising from the concentration of U.S. military power in Vietnam and the presence of a CPR confrontation with the Soviet Union. . . ." [33] The coup's failure, Malik concluded, "meant the liberation of Indonesia from CPR domination in the ideological field, which in turn meant the liberation of Indonesia from communist dictatorship and personality cult." Thus, the new

[30] ANTARA, April 15, 1967.
[31] ANTARA, April 27, 1967.
[32] NCNA, April 30, 1967.
[33] Djakarta Domestic Service, May 17, 1967.

Indonesian government had reversed China's role from major ally to major enemy and, as Malik's press conference implied, it was also engaged in reevaluating its concomitant ties with other major Asian power centers.

CRITICISMS OF PEKING'S PRE-COUP POLICY OF COOPERATION WITH INDONESIA

The post-coup destruction of the PKI and Indonesia's inexorable about-face in foreign policy were bound to lead to recrimination both within the Chinese wing of the communist bloc and within the CPR power elite itself. The ostensible focal point of these reproaches was the PKI, particularly its internal organization and policy of revolution from above, that is, reliance upon Sukarno's good will. However, there was also another possible focal point—that segment of the CCP leadership which could be blamed for supporting the Aidit-Sukarno relationship. This focus became manifest only after the Great Cultural Revolution began and Maoist ire was directed at Peng Chen and Liu Shao-chi, both of whom had been associated with China's Indonesian policy.

It is worth noting that neither the Chinese nor the Indonesian communists could have been unaware of the difficulties of conducting guerrilla warfare in Indonesia. It was apparent that the PKI lacked secure rural bases such as communist groups possessed in China, Laos, and Vietnam. Nor did Indonesia have a frontier with a bloc country. Finally, the PKI could not even hope to utilize the outer islands, for its own organization was weakest there and that of anti-communist Indonesian groups strongest. As if environmental problems were not enough, Aidit himself complained just four months before the coup that the party's organizational structure was breaking down and that communication links between the leadership and rank-and-file party members had become entangled. He lamented almost prophetically: "The slowness in executing the party's decisions shows that leadership methods have not been improved. If this weakness is not corrected soon, it will bring great disaster." [34] Certainly the inability of the party to muster its reserves in the first days of October might be attributed in part to this organizational lag which Aidit was bewailing.

In one of the most ingenuous postmortems to come out of the bloc countries, Czech media tried to balance blame with praise of the PKI, which prior to the coup "remained the only force which consistently unmasked corruption and sharply attacked all those who were enriching themselves by embezzling." However, the party had become overconfident as it began to move into policymaking circles, a development which gave its enemies the chance to place some of the onus of blame for Indonesia's problems on the PKI. Moreover, Radio Prague pointed out that "the party leadership cooperated with the hated Chinese minority." Thus, considerable animosity toward the PKI existed in the Indonesian environment, enough to require only an excuse to wreak havoc upon the party. Such an excuse was more than provided by the massacre of the generals. The party's destruction "shows that leftist extremism is an immense danger to any progressive movement" because it "delivers its supporters to the tender mercies of the attacking enemy." [35]

While Czech media were evenhanded in their treatment of the PKI, other communist parties launched small-scale polemics of their own over the Indonesian events. The pro-

[34] Aidit, *Report to Fourth Plenum,* May 11, 1965, in JPRS, *Translations on South and East Asia,* 91 (August 9, 1965): 67.
[35] Prague Domestic Service, October 9, 1966.

Peking splinter of the Belgian communist party in its weekly *La Voix du Peuple* on January 20 and 27, 1967, chose to defend PKI actions against "trotskyite" charges that its united front policy was in fact "class collaboration, a subordination of the labor movement to the so-called national bourgeoisie." Instead, the paper stressed the importance of "knowing whom the armed forces served" for determining the class character of a state." According to the account in *La Voix du Peuple* of an alleged PKI Politburo self-criticism dated August 17, 1966, the party attributed its defeat to the "theory of two aspects in state power"—the pro- and anti-people aspects—which "caused the proletariat to be taken in tow by the national bourgeoisie." The self-criticism stated that the PKI erred in believing that the state machinery (perhaps a reference to the military) "would be 'above' or 'outside the classes.' "

The dissident Belgian socialist weekly *La Gauche,* on the other hand, ascribed the PKI failure to "leftist" and "adventurist . . . insurrection" rather than "opportunistic errors of accommodations to the 'national' middle class." It accused the pro-Peking Belgian communist party of lamely trying to defend the Maoist theory of a united front by blaming the machinations of U.S. imperialism for the PKI defeat. "When it is a question of a communist party which claims to have three million members and twelve million sympathizers, the excuse of a concurrence of unfavorable forces can obviously not be used." [36]

The PKI self-criticism referred to by *La Voix du Peuple* was first released in summary form by Albanian media in May 1967 and then in full by NCNA on July 7 and 8, 1967, almost one year after it had been published in installments in the *Indonesian Tribune*—apparently the voice of the new

[36] See the exchange in JPRS, *Translations on International Communist Developments,* nos. 949, 950 (1967), *passim.*

Peking-based PKI—in November 1966 (its first issue) and January 1967.[37] The self-criticism is a particularly interesting document, not because it gives any particular insight into the PKI motives and decisions which led to the coup, but rather for its distortions of pre-coup party policy and its relations with the CPR. In disseminating the self-criticism, Peking was apparently trying to get off the hook as the PKI's pre-coup mentor and to shift the responsibility for the debacle onto the CPSU. In other words, the self-criticism became one more aspect of the Sino-Soviet dispute. (Predictably, Moscow has not discussed the substance of the "self-criticism," at least to this author's knowledge.)

The self-criticism begins by noting that "due to the absence of the working class leadership, the Republic of Indonesia was inevitably a state ruled by the bourgeoisie, despite the participation of the proletariat" and that "it was a great mistake to assume that the existence of such a government signified a fundamental change in the class character of the state power . . . or of a pro-people aspect within the state power." Action on the basis of this theory had "dissolved the interests of the proletariat in that of the national bourgeoisie" leading to "the growth of right apostatism which merged with the influence of modern revisionism in the international communist movement." Thus, by simply ignoring the fact that the CCP had encouraged PKI cooperation with Sukarno as part of its own alliance policy, the document attempts to shift the blame onto the CPSU.

The document claims that modern revisionism came into the party after 1951, that is, after Aidit had assumed leadership:

---

[37] The following discussion of the statement is based on the NCNA texts. Moscow did not acknowledge the "self-criticism" until March 1968 in a broadcast accusing those who wrote it of being "Indonesian Maoists who have found refuge in Peking." See Moscow Radio in Mandarin, March 8, 1968.

Modern revisionism began to come into the party when the fourth plenary session of the Central Committee of the Fifth Congress uncritically approved a report which supported the line of the 20th CPSU Congress and adopted the line of achieving socialism peacefully through parliamentary means. . . . Such a stand did not emanate from the independent interests of the proletariat but rather from the need to save the alliance with the nation's bourgeoisie.

The PKI . . . made concessions in the theoretical field, wanting to make Marxism, which is the ideology of the working class, the property of the whole nation, which includes the exploiting classes hostile to the working class.

Chiding Aidit for his insistence that the PKI path was *sui generis,* and independent of both the CPSU and CCP, the document takes issue with his claim that "the 'two aspect theory' was completely different from the 'theory of structural reform' of the leadership of the revisionist Italian Communist Party. However, the fact is . . . there is no difference between the two 'theories.' " The document reflects the fact that eight years of Sukarno's tutelage had not advanced the PKI cause but rather had served to domesticate the party, which mistook the president's radical vocabulary for a commitment to Marxism-Leninism. In fact, the party had been forced to inhibit its campaign against private and government enterprise in order to fit Sukarno's syncretic conservatism which was designed to sustain support from such antagonistic groups as the military and Moslem landlords on the one hand and the PKI on the other. Sukarno's co-optation of the PKI served to dull its fangs, at least until the party's 1964 decision to initiate unilaterally through the BTI its land reform program. Such action broke the bonds of mutual tolerance and through 1964–65 led to a number of violent confrontations in Central and East Java between the Moslem landholding elements and the rural proletariat.[38] According to the NCNA text: "In many articles and speeches, the party leaders frequently said that the struggle of the PKI was based not only on Marxism-Leninism but also on 'the teachings of Sukarno' [which led to] the erroneous view that 'to implement MANIPOL in a consistent manner is the same as implementing the program of the PKI.'" It is likely that Peking was implicitly comparing the errors of the PKI to its own near-fatal policy of cooperation with Chiang Kai-shek prior to the 1927 march north, the parallel being that just as Chiang turned against the CCP so Sukarno either wittingly or because he lacked the power permitted the military to destroy the PKI.

As for the party's failure in the coup aftermath, the self-criticism points to the erroneous policy of expanding party membership to "work in the united front with the national bourgeoisie and to supply various cadres in the state institutions that were obtained thanks to cooperation with the national bourgeoisie," rather than providing Marxist-Leninist training to prepare the cadres "for work among the peasants in order to establish revolutionary bases." The document concludes by admitting that the party has been decimated and that the only opportunity for its renaissance is to cleave to "the inexorable law that the main force of the people's democratic revolution in Indonesia is the peasantry and its base area is the countryside."

The two most important purposes of the Peking-directed PKI self-flagellation were: (1) to dissociate the CCP from the PKI's popular front policy of the Sukarno period and (2) indirectly to refute the propaganda campaign of the Indonesian military that the CCP had helped plan the coup.

---

[38] See the interesting discussion in W. F. Wertheim, "Indonesia Before and After the Untung Coup," *Pacific Affairs*, 39, nos. 1 and 2 (Spring–Summer, 1966).

By castigating the notion of cooperation in any group which would not be led by the party, the self-criticism, in effect, argues that the CCP would never back a scheme, like Untung's, which would have relegated the PKI to the role of minor partner in a military-led coalition.

*   *   *

The impact of a foreign policy setback or adverse change in a state's international environment on the internal affairs of that state depends on how well the psychological and organizational boundaries of the state are defended. The CPR organizational structure was probably insulated enough to absorb the setback of a break in the Sino-Indonesian alliance, and even the destruction of the PKI. Psychologically, however, this foreign policy setback coincided with the most severe internal upheaval ever to have occurred since the CCP came to power in 1949. It was inevitable that a fiasco as great as the October 1965 Indonesian coup attempt would affect the Chinese internal power and value struggle known as the Great Cultural Revolution and that such figures as Liu Shao-chi and Peng Chen would make convenient scapegoats for the regime's foreign policy failures. Their fumbling in the foreign policy field would be portrayed as the logical outcome of their domestic revisionism. Thus, a foreign policy setback for China brought about by events beyond Peking's control could be rationalized away as the product of internal betrayal by dissenters within the CCP's own ranks rather than as an adversary's strength. As Lewis Coser puts it in a proposition that could explain in part the severity of the Great Cultural Revolution: "[Whereas] a flexible society benefits from conflict behavior inasmuch as this behavior through the creation and modification of norms, assures its continuance under changed conditions, a rigid system, on the other hand, by not permitting conflict, will impede needed adjustments and so maximize the danger of catastrophic breakdown." [39]

To put the proposition another way: a totalitarian system with a monolithic ideology, like China, may so distort the data received from its environment that major foreign policy setbacks cannot readily be accepted without challenging the efficacy of the ideology and ultimately the legitimacy of the regime. Thus, when policy failures must be acknowledged, they are likely to be personalized and labeled products of conspiracy rather than the results of events beyond the state's control.[40]

There is little doubt that Chinese differences with such hitherto strongly pro-Peking communist parties as the Japan Communist Party (JCP) and the Korean Workers Party (KWP) surfaced in the aftermath of the Indonesian coup. These parties decided to pursue a more independent course of action when they perceived that the PKI received no aid from Peking during its time of need. Thus, the coup called into question the CCP's position of leadership within the radical wing of international communism and led to, if not a realignment with the CPSU on the part of the JCP and the KWP, at least a notable moderation of their views. Instead of attempting to meliorate its own policies, however, the CCP, caught in the throes of the GCR, has excommunicated the JCP and has been somewhat cool in its relations with the KWP as well during 1966–67.

As for its Indonesian policy failure, Chinese media lay the blame squarely on Liu Shao-chi. Condemning his 1963 visit to Indonesia, they claim that he "spread the bourgeois line on foreign affairs, attacked the CCP's foreign policy, prettified the bourgeois politician Sukarno, opposed Chairman Mao,

[39] Lewis Coser, *The Functions of Social Conflict* (Glencoe, Ill.: The Free Press, 1956), p. 128.
[40] See, for example, Farrell, "Foreign Policies of Open and Closed Political Societies," in his *Approaches to Comparative and International Politics* (Evanston: Northwestern University Press, 1966), p. 176.

and advocated 'peaceful coexistence' and 'peaceful transition.' " [41] The Peking press linked Liu's revisionist stature
abroad to his alleged counterrevolutionary activities at home
and asserted that just as he "highly praised the PKI's policy
of class collaboration . . . in the 'NASAKOM' road," so he
also "carried out intensive activities to restore capitalism in
China." [42]

What augured worse for the accuracy of future Chinese
diplomatic information-gathering activities was the following
admonition to CPR "diplomatic fighters" in a *People's Daily*
editorial: "We will never barter away either our principles
or the interests of the people of other countries. Our
diplomatic fighters will never praise the bourgeoisie in an
unprincipled way or curry favor with them." [43] The implication of this order seems clearly to require that diplomatic
analysis be confined to the potential weaknesses and vulnera-
bilities of a host country and not consider its strengths or
the progress it is making. If such a steady diet of distorted
information is not offset by other sources, not only will
Peking misperceive the world outside its boundaries but,
more importantly, it will perceive that world to be much
more ripe for direct Chinese subversion or attack than, in
fact, it is.

A NEW PEKING-BACKED PKI

The table in Chapter Six which shows Chinese perceptions
of Indonesia in the post-coup period indicates that through
December 1967 only thirteen commentaries dealt with the
necessity of a new PKI, a theme which was not initiated
by the Chinese until some seven months after the coup
attempt. Despite their paucity in number, however, the
substance of these comments is enlightening in that it indi-

[41] Peking Domestic Service, July 13, 1967, and *People's Daily,* July 13, 1967.
[42] *People's Daily,* October 12, 1967, and *Liberation Army Daily,* December 4,
1967.
[43] *People's Daily* editorial, June 28, 1967.

cates what sort of party the Maoists would like to create as an overseas model for the export of their own GCR.

As discussed earlier, Chinese treatment of the PKI after the coup refused to acknowledge that the party had ground to a halt as an operating political entity. Peking's initial references in April 1966, to party activities, as distinct from reports of atrocities visited upon the party, were in reprints of Albanian and North Vietnamese articles encouraging the inauguration of a "just, revolutionary struggle" against the military. Carrying in full the statement of the Peking-based Thai Communist Party, Peking insisted that the "only way to the victory of a revolution is to follow steadfastly the road of armed struggle." [44] A summary of a pro-Peking New Zealand Communist Party resolution the same month interpreted Indonesian developments as exposing the "utter fallacy of revisionist theories of peaceful transition to socialism." Implicitly criticizing the PKI for subordinating itself to NASAKOM, it warned, "unless the working class has the leadership in a national liberation revolution, the transformation of such a revolution into a socialist revolution will inevitably come up against the opposition of a compromising section of the national bourgeoisie." [45] In the first reference carried by Chinese media to the party's future, the resolution noted cryptically that "the PKI is developing new organizational forms."

Following up on these introductions, the "new" PKI allegedly sent a message to the New Zealand party in April which declared with unconscious irony that the PKI had "lifted the struggle of the Indonesian people . . . to a new level, the level of a long and complicated struggle." No longer would the party accept a coalition arrangement with the ruling class, because "events in Indonesia have proved once again that there is no dominating class which voluntarily

[44] NCNA, April 9, 1966.
[45] Ibid., April 19, 1966.

relinquishes its power." The message was signed simply "the delegation from the central committee of the PKI" with no names appended.[46] Indonesian officials were not unaware of these developments. Foreign Minister Malik, in an April press conference, stated that the Indonesian government anticipated the creation of a new Peking-based PKI modeled after the Thai Communist party, perhaps led by former Indonesian Ambassador to the CPR, Djawoto.[47]

Albania provided the first systematic projection of what the characteristics of a new PKI should be—a projection later endorsed in all its essentials by the CPR. In a lengthy article in the party press, Tirana acknowledged that the party was in "grave danger" and had but "one alternative—to reply to counterrevolutionary violence by revolutionary violence." Warning the party against hewing to earlier revisionist lines, Tirana declared that the PKI's error lay in putting "too much faith in the political strength of Sukarno . . . whose prestige did not lie on any solid base and in trusting NASAKOM, an institution which in the last analysis was still controlled by non and anticommunist groups." [48] The Albanian critique of the PKI could well have been leveled against the CCP which had, through late 1964 and 1965, offered considerable propaganda support to the PKI's pressure for NASAKOM. If the Indonesian party had erred in relying on Sukarno, so had the Chinese party in its alliance with Indonesia and its endorsement of the PKI's peaceful penetration program—a mistake, discussed above, which the Maoists have tried to pin exclusively on Liu Shao-chi and his followers during the course of the GCR.

Perhaps because of the infighting among CCP factions, Peking did not come up with an authoritative analysis of PKI faults for some months after the Albanian statement.

[46] Carried in *Zeri I Popullit,* May 5, 1966.
[47] *Duta Masjarakat,* April 21, 1966, in JPRS, *Translations on South and East Asia,* vol. 113 (May 13, 1966), and ANTARA, July 18, 1966.
[48] *Zeri I Popullit,* May 12, 1966.

Nonetheless, the Chinese made their general position known by publicizing the statements of such front groups as the Afro-Asian Writers Conference whose acting secretary-general Ibrahim Isa (long associated with Sukarno's confrontation policy and the Peking-backed Malayan National Liberation League) stated that: "For the Indonesian people who are today struggling against the counterrevolutionaries headed by Nasution and Suharto, there is only one road leading toward victory, that is, the road of revolution pointed out by Chairman Mao Tse-tung. For the Indonesian people, the road toward victory is the road of Mao Tse-tung." [49]

In a general foreign policy discussion in late 1966, a Chinese correspondent reported that the Indonesian people "are now reorganizing their ranks and beginning to meet counterrevolutionary arms with revolutionary arms," a prospect which had been acknowledged by official Indonesia when the Djakarta military commander General Machmud warned that only thirty-one PKI central committee members had been captured or killed, leaving thirty-five at large—surely enough to recreate a new party apparatus.[50] Some seven hundred "Gestapu-PKI fugitives" were estimated by Indonesian sources to be in Peking.[51]

It is undoubtedly this nucleus in Peking that has created the new publication, *Indonesian Tribune*, although the location of its publication has not been mentioned by Chinese media. Despite the strong probability of the publication's Chinese origin, Albania, once again, was the first pro-Peking party or state to announce its existence and report its contents.[52] A January 1967 ATA summary of the paper's first issue, "published recently," stated that "Indonesian communists have reorganized themselves" and are learning through "serious self-criticism" the revisionist errors of the

[49] NCNA, July 30, 1966, and March 20, 1967.
[50] *Ibid.*, December 29, 1966, and ANTARA, August 4, 1966.
[51] Djakarta Domestic Service, November 22, 1966.
[52] Tirana, ATA (Albanian Press Service), January 7, 1967.

past. A so-called Politburo declaration of August 17, 1966, is cited formulating the "urgent tasks" of the party as "creation of a united front *under PKI leadership* [emphasis added] and the development of armed struggle . . . to overthrow the fascist regime of Suharto-Nasution."

Finally, in July 1967, Peking issued its first authoritative analysis of the PKI's future program in the eleventh issue of *Red Flag*. An editorial devoted exclusively to the PKI stated at the outset: "The people of Indonesia are determined to make revolution. And the Chinese people are determined to support their revolution." The article implied, however, that such support would be more hortatory than practical and that the party was still concerned with "regrouping." Quoting from the supposed August 17, 1966, self-criticism, *Red Flag* emphasized: "To achieve complete victory the Indonesian revolution must take the road of the Chinese revolution . . . the armed agrarian revolution of the peasants under the leadership of the proletariat." As for the PKI's pre-coup strategy which followed "the revisionist road of 'peaceful transition' advocated by the leadership of the CPSU," subsequent events proved that it is "the road to burying the revolution and the road to exterminating the party and the people." Repudiating the attempts to struggle simultaneously within the armed forces and in the countryside and the city, *Red Flag* urged the party to emulated Mao by "establishing revolutionary base areas and turning the backward villages into strong, consolidated, military, political, and cultural bastions of the revolution." Thus, the CCP recognized the fact that the PKI/BTI had helped to create class consciousness in the countryside and that such indigenous sources of unrest as land hunger and tenant farming in Java would still be available for organized political exploitation since the current Indonesian regime had discontinued even Sukarno's limited agrarian reform program.

Concluding with a warning and a hope for a reconstituted

Maoist PKI, *Red Flag* succinctly summed up the problems such a complete reversal of strategy would entail:

> The PKI is faced with an extremely difficult and complex task. The party's struggle is undergoing a major change: a switch from the cities to the countryside, from peaceful struggle to armed struggle, from legal to illegal, from open to secret. It is indeed not easy for a party, which for so long carried on principally open and legal activity in the cities, to make this switch effective. It is bound to meet with many difficulties. But the objective realities of the revolutionary struggle will compel people to make the change, compel them to master armed struggle, and there is no alternative but for them to master it.

In effect, the CCP called upon the PKI to return to a conspiratorial cadre party instead of relying on nominal mass membership. It called upon the party to stop honoring the rules of Sukarno's political game which, in any case, had been stopped when Suharto became acting president in March 1966 and to return to the role of revolutionary party outside the regime and dedicated to its overthrow.

What remains of the PKI, then, seems to have become a CCP satellite. In exchange for asylum, PKI remnants in Peking have apparently subscribed to a pure Maoist program designed more for the internal politics of the Great Cultural Revolution than for practical Chinese foreign policy. In fact, Peking has lost its influence connections in Indonesia: the alliance is broken and pro-Peking Indonesian personnel from the Sukarno government have been incarcerated. What is more, the PKI, on whom the CCP relied to penetrate below the official level of the Indonesian polity, lies decimated. The voice of a reorganized PKI, mentioned in the *Red Flag*, takes on the hollow sound of braggadocio. Subservient to internal Chinese politics, the PKI seems in a poor position to further its prospects as a radical Indonesian party.

Conclusion: Indonesia's Realignment Pattern
and China's Objections

Up to this point I have been concerned with explicating
the Sino-Indonesian entente as a kind of Chinese "informal
penetration" of Indonesia, and with the impact of the abortive coup on disrupting this relationship both on a state-to-
state basis and with respect to Peking's major nongovernmental agent, the PKI. In this chapter, I shall broaden my
focus to encompass Indonesia's "realignment" in international
politics, as well as the Suharto regime's restructuring of the
domestic political process, for the purpose of delineating the
CPR's reaction to its most grievous foreign policy setback
since the U.S.S.R.'s refusal to back its attempt to seize the
offshore islands in the late 1950's. It is hoped that an analysis
of China's response to Indonesian developments will give us
some insight into Peking's perceptions of the external environment when it is clearly interpreted as hostile rather
than benign, and give us some notion of how Peking actually
behaves in such a situation. The advantage of the case study
approach taken in this manuscript lies in its ability to show
how the parameters of likely choices are actually narrowed
by policy-makers operating in the real world, rather than by
academicians constructing choice models which may or may

not apply to any given case. As for the ability to generalize from the Sino-Indonesian case or to construct hypotheses of general Chinese foreign policy behavior, it seems to me that we may be able to suggest something along the line of the negative predictions mentioned by Bruce Russett; that is, through the case study approach, it is plausible "to narrow the range of possibilities, to eliminate some events as unlikely, and to produce a range of outcomes within which future developments will lie." [1] In other words, a case study can show us how Peking perceives and reacts to a given situation, and the options it both employs and discards. A series of such studies, provided there are pre-established criteria of comparability, could help us to create a profile of Chinese foreign policy behavior. Such a profile could help us to predict future Chinese action on any current issue by comparing Peking's perceptions of the issue with perceptions of past cases and then analyzing whether the behavior manifested in the past would be plausible in the current case. The obvious caveat in such a framework, of course, is the fact that new variables are constantly entering the decision-making apparatus. To cite just two in the Chinese case, the acquisition of thermonuclear capability might well be perceived as providing extra psychological leverage on Asian states; on the other hand, the bureaucratic and military disruption created by the GCR might lead foreign policy decision-makers to pull in their horns. In any event, a careful series of case studies of Chinese foreign policy with the goal of creating typologies could help noncommunist analysts of Chinese affairs increase the accuracy of their predictions of Chinese behavior.

CESSATION OF *Konfrontasi*

To turn back now from the level of general proposition to that of case study, we shall examine Peking's perception of,

[1] Bruce M. Russett, "The Ecology of Future International Politics," *International Studies Quarterly,* 11, no. 1 (March, 1967): 13.

and reactions to, a number of Indonesian foreign policy initiatives in the post-coup period as well as its shift in internal elites. One of the first foreign policy changes adopted by the Suharto government was the move toward a settlement of *Konfrontasi*, a posture to which the military had given only lukewarm support from the beginning. As a military–civilian/technocratic group moved into power under Suharto's aegis, a new image system developed which led to the following sequence: (*a*) Indonesia's new leaders no longer felt threatened by Malaysia and vice versa; (*b*) Indonesia's new leaders redefined their goals toward the region and concluded: (*c*) that "Konfrontasi" was a waste of resources desperately needed for other tasks; (*d*) Indonesian attention shifted to a new opponent—China. The importance of this last development for an understanding of the new Indonesian government is that it has not broken so completely from the Sukarno past as many superficial observers have concluded. The Suharto government seeks national support and rationalizes weaknesses of the regime by arguing, just as Sukarno did, the exigencies of encirclement. Instead of NEKOLIM, the new devils are China and communism, and they are similarly being used to justify the maintenance of inflated military budgets which in 1965 may have reached as high as 70 per cent of the total budget.[2] Suharto's decision to stop confronting Malaysia and begin confronting the CPR has led him to search for new allies, a difficult task in that he simultaneously desires to refurbish the country's nonaligned image.

Malaysia enthusiastically welcomed the Indonesian shift. Authorities in Kuala Lumpur were particularly gratified with Indonesian cooperation in closing down the Djakarta-based, Free Malaysia movement and in enjoining Azahari from using Indonesian facilities for propaganda. According to

[2] *New York Times*, February 5, 1967.

one analyst, Malaysian officials, in private, even discussed prospects for a Malaysian-Singapore-Indonesian arrangement against an expansionist CPR. (This will be discussed later.)[3]

Peking was cognizant of Indonesian moves to end confrontation, and in the spring of 1966 it commented on them in the broader framework of implementing a "reactionary foreign policy of fraternizing with the United States, associating with the Soviet Union, and opposing China," as well as "stepping up collusion" with Malaysia, Japan, and India. In effect, Peking was placing Indonesia in the company of its regional and global adversaries.[4]

As confrontation came to an end after the May 1966 Bangkok conference, the Indonesian press for the first time carried accounts that Great Britain had been planning for a number of years to reduce its commitments in Southeast Asia and quoted then Foreign Secretary Stewart's remark that "the stationing of British troops anywhere in the world would not be in conflict with the interests of both sides." [5] Despite Sukarno's insistence in late July that "Confrontation goes on," by mid-August Indonesia and Malaysia had re-established diplomatic ties. Eschewing any mention of Sukarno, who by this time had become a political nonentity in Peking's eyes, the Chinese depicted the Indonesian-Malaysian rapprochement as the action of two satellites "of U.S. and British imperialism." [6]

Chinese officials were concerned not only by the cessation of Indonesian-Malaysian hostilities but more importantly by the rapid moves of the two states toward military cooperation, measures which Peking interpreted as part of a broader

[3] René Peritz, "The Changing World of Malaysia," Current History, 52, no. 305 (January, 1967): 33; Justus M. Van der Kroef, "Chinese Minority Aspirations and Problems in Sarawak," Pacific Affairs, 39, nos. 1, 2 (Spring–Summer, 1966): 79–80.
[4] NCNA, May 10, 1966.
[5] ANTARA, July 2, 1966.
[6] NCNA, August 12, 1966.

American-initiated China-containment policy. Peking media reported the establishment of a joint Indonesian-Malaysian military mission in early September, "to carry out armed suppression jointly . . . against the people of Kalimantan." [7] The brunt of any combined border control operation in North Borneo would in large part be directed against the predominantly Chinese, Clandestine Communist Organization (CCO) of Sarawak, a number of whose members had been trained in Indonesia and then infiltrated back across the border. If a suppression operation proved successful, Peking's influence would further diminish among the Overseas Chinese, who would see it as another instance of the CPR's inability to protect them and would realize the ineffectiveness of Maoist guerrilla tactics where secure rural redoubts are unavailable.

By the spring of 1967, the Malaysian-Indonesian relationship had become close enough that Peking felt compelled to fulminate against a suggestion attributed to the Sumatra military commander, Mokoginta, that Malaysia form a "military alliance" with Indonesia and other Southeast Asian states "to meet 'the threat from China.' " [8] As an earnest of Indonesia's good intentions toward Malaysia, it is noteworthy that the Sabah elections in April were attended by a *pro forma* group of Indonesian observers who agreed to accept the results of these regular elections as evidence of Sabah's desire to remain within the federation, even though this was not an election issue.[9] Malaysian authorities had suggested this procedure a number of times during *Konfrontasi* as a face-saving way to break the impasse, but Sukarno had refused. With the change of Indonesian ruling elites, Suharto eagerly accepted this solution.

[7] *Ibid.*, September 5, 1966.
[8] *Ibid.*, March 30, 1967.
[9] See the *New York Times,* April 9, 1967.

INDONESIAN COOPERATION WITH THE UNITED STATES AND SOVIET UNION

As discussed in the preceding section, Peking perceived the end of confrontation and the establishment of Malay-Indonesian ties to be a coordinated Western strategy directed against China. In fact, the United States has been able to establish a good diplomatic relationship with the Suharto government, oriented toward economic rehabilitation and toward a change in foreign policy away from Sukarno's radical nationalist pseudo-neutrality to the benevolent neutrality characterized by Malaysia. A recent manifestation of the new relationship was exhibited in publishing the full text of U.S. Ambassador Green's July 4 address in which he praised Indonesia's "realistic stabilization program" and assured the Indonesian government of America's continued assistance of up to one-third of its 1967 foreign exchange needs.[10] Suharto's apparent willingness to trust the United States is due in part to the latter's policy of aloofness toward Sukarno during the last few years of his regime. This policy has made the United States a more acceptable associate. Conversely, Suharto's caution toward the U.S.S.R. may be explained by that nation's vigorous backing of Sukarno, and by its public condemnation of Suharto's policies of destroying the PKI and forbidding the dissemination of communist propaganda. On the other hand, it would by no means be inconsistent for the U.S.S.R. to inaugurate a new aid program to Indonesia based on the same premises as its aid to India, Pakistan, and Egypt —counteraction of American influence, encouragement of independence from "imperialism," and the strengthening of potential future adversaries of China. In fact, Moscow has tried to put the best face on Indonesian foreign policy by emphasizing Indonesian statements which insist that the state

[10] See the *Indonesian Observer*, July 7, 1967.

"will continue its independent and active foreign policy in the struggle against imperialism and colonialism." [11]

Peking's propaganda attack on Indonesia's new orientation toward the United States did not begin until the summer of 1966 in response to Secretary of State Rusk's announcement that the 1967 foreign aid program would once more include Indonesia. Peking admonished that the "U.S. imperialists" were "dreaming . . . of wresting away and revoking Indonesian national independence and making Indonesia one of their satellites . . . to suppress the national liberation movement." [12] The press warned Indonesia, in a typical example of Chinese Cold War mentality: "It has become a law in international class struggles that one who is pro-United States inevitably opposes China and one who opposes China is bound to go over completely to U.S. imperialism." [13]

Apprehensive over prospects for a combined U.S.–Soviet assistance program, Radio Peking stressed to its Indonesian leftist audience that Soviet weapons were employed in the PKI massacre and that Indonesian officials were begging simultaneously from Washington and Moscow.[14] Peking capitalized on any incident which could be interpreted as evidence of a link between the U.S., the U.S.S.R., and Indonesia, or between the two former and the latter. Thus, when Anwar Dharma, the *Harian Rakjat* correspondent, was expelled from Moscow in September 1966, for " 'engaging in anti-Soviet activities and maintaining an active contact with a certain foreign mission which is hostile to the Soviet Union,' " Chinese media interpreted the expulsion as further evidence of "the intimate cooperation between the Soviet modern revisionists and the fascist military regime of Indonesia . . . taken at a time when Djakarta was busy arrang-

---

[11] Moscow Radio in Indonesian, August 22, 1966.
[12] Peking Radio in Indonesian, August 3, 1966.
[13] *People's Daily* Commentator, August 17, 1966.
[14] Peking Radio in Indonesian, September 6, 1966; NCNA, September 5, 1966; *People's Daily*, September 11, 1966.

ing the visit of Adam Malik . . . to the Soviet Union."
Citing a statement by Dharma, who was granted asylum in
the CPR, Peking quoted his charge against Brezhnev and
the CPSU Central Committee that "in their lectures before
the masses in residential districts, institutes, and universities,
when speaking about the present Indonesian situation, they
have never failed to launch slanderous accusations against
the PKI whom they called the tail end of Peking." [15]

Inadvertently reinforcing this Chinese interpretation, Djakarta's own commentators in assessing Malik's visit to the
Soviet Union pointed out that Soviet-Indonesian relations
had been hampered in the past by Chinese attempts to use
the PKI against such ties. "With the destruction of the PKI
. . . , however, the CPR pressure group disappeared and
the chance emerged to improve Indonesian-Soviet relations." [16] Moscow seemed to accept this explanation in its
own accusations against China over the CCP's adverse impact
on the PKI. Reviewing past Chinese efforts to foster policies
of "weakening cooperation between Indonesia and the Soviet
Union" and encouraging "adventurism" by the PKI—only
to back off after the coup—Moscow charged the Chinese with
gross hypocrisy: "We would like to point out . . . that at
that time the Peking leaders worked harder than anybody
else in the world in praising Sukarno and lauding his vain
statements. . . . The Maoists felt that it would thus be
easier to place Indonesia under their influence." [17]

In order to legitimize its opposition to Suharto's new foreign policy, the CPR employed certain Indonesian-exile
groups as its spokesmen. Thus, the Peking-based "Federation
of Indonesian Students in China" issued a statement "denouncing the Soviet modern revisionist clique for its betrayal
of the Indonesian people" by openly aiding the Suharto

[15] NCNA, October 5, 1966.
[16] Radio Djakarta, October 20, 1966.
[17] Moscow Radio in Mandarin, August 6, 1967.

regime to suppress the PKI. Revealing the Chinese hand behind the "Federation," the statement stressed that the Soviet
leaders "have never denounced the anti-China racist acts, but
shield the Suharto-Nasution regime in its abuse of the
Chinese. They have never renounced the pro-U.S. policy
pursued by the Suharto-Nasution regime, but instead describe
it as anti-imperialist." [18]

Perhaps in response to these Chinese charges and ostensibly in response to Indonesian claims that the U.S.S.R. con-
doned the PKI slaughter, *Pravda* declared: "The fact that the
Soviet Union maintains interstate relations with Indonesia
does not mean that anyone in the Soviet socialist state can
remain indifferent to terrorist acts against communists, the
ban on the PKI, and persecution of Marxist-Leninist ideology." All of these, *Pravda* maintained, "were angrily condemned by the Soviet people" (although apparently *not* by
Soviet officials). As for the future, *Pravda* said: "Soviet policy
is to support the Indonesian course toward national independence in the face of imperialist powers." [19] Although
embarrassed by Suharto's domestic anticommunism, the Soviets were not about to let this policy interfere with state
relations as was indicated when the U.S.S.R. agreed to reschedule Indonesia's debt payments after Malik's November
1966 visit. The U.S.S.R. was simply following the same
strategy it had used in dealing with such states as Egypt and
India, that is, separating the treatment of indigenous communist parties from government-to-government relations. In
those states the U.S.S.R. considered important as buffers
against China and/or the United States, it has been prepared
to sacrifice local communist ambitions for Soviet national
ends. The new Indonesian regime was quick to encourage
Soviet concessions by claiming that instead of impairing relations with the U.S.S.R., "the consequence of our successful

[18] NCNA, November 12, 1966.
[19] *Pravda* editorial, November 23, 1966.

crushing of the Gestapu-PKI affair last year is the restoration
of our friendship with such countries as the Soviet Union." [20]
Moscow was not pleased, however, with the Western con-
sortium organized by Djakarta's noncommunist creditors to
reschedule Indonesian debts and internationalize new credit
arrangements. Radio Moscow warned that "the so-called
Tokyo club . . . will mean a collective supervision of the
Indonesian economy by Western countries under leadership
of the United States." [21]

Predictably, Peking viewed Djakarta's acceptance of both
the American and Soviet initiatives as sellouts, the *People's
Daily* charging that the United States and the Soviet Union
colluded in Indonesia "to fabricate rumors and slanders
against China." The paper looked askance at the alleged
"intensified military collusion between the Soviet revisionists
and the Indonesian reactionaries as shown by continued shipments of military equipment to Indonesia and frequent
meetings between high-ranking military officers of the two
countries." [22] Refuting Moscow's "sham opposition" to the
Suharto government's destruction of the PKI, the *People's
Daily* asked rhetorically why, if it is so opposed to the new
regime, does the Soviet Union praise Suharto as a fighter
against imperialism and continue to supply him with economic and military aid? [23] As for the United States, it asserted
that the Indonesian government's new foreign investment
laws will "turn Indonesia into a U.S. colony." [24]

Just as the United States was able to establish its creden-
tials with Suharto because it dissociated itself from his predecessor, so the Soviet Union appeared to be employing the
same tactic when in March 1967 it linked Sukarno with the
1965 coup attempt by reporting some of the Mahmilub

[20] Djakarta Domestic Service, November 24, 1966.
[21] Moscow Radio in Indonesian, January 25, 1967.
[22] *People's Daily,* March 23, 1967.
[23] *Ibid.,* April 4, 1967.
[24] NCNA, April 8, 1967.

testimony from the Subandrio, Untung, and Njono trials. The Soviet press charged that "Sukarno began to oppose the idea of peaceful coexistence and . . . slipped into dangerous adventures. He led Indonesia out of the United Nations . . . and declared the so-called 'confrontation' with Malaysia to be the country's main task, which consumed up to 80 percent of the annual state budget. *The Peking leaders incited the states one against the other, and the confrontation pleased them.*" [25] (Emphasis added.) Moscow, in effect, was simply reiterating Suharto's own interpretation of Sukarno's foreign policy and Peking's role in its formulation. Looking to the future, Moscow once more offered its hand to Suharto by stating: "If . . . the statements of the present leaders on the nonalignment with blocs are implemented and if these leaders do not permit their country to be dragged into the sphere of imperialist influence, Indonesia will succeed in occupying a worthy place in the modern world." [26]

Indonesian attempts to maintain relations with the Asian wing of the bloc and Peking-oriented Cambodia had mixed results, probably determined by the degree of independence each felt it exercised vis-à-vis Peking. Hanoi, from the beginning, castigated the Suharto government almost as vigorously as did Peking. Pyongyang, on the other hand, did not comment on Indonesian events and maintained "correct," if not overly cordial, relations. As for Cambodia, Suharto apparently hoped to sustain his ties with Phnom Penh as evidence of Indonesia's continued adherence to nonalignment. Sihanouk, however, probably feared the effect of guilt-by-association if he built new links with a state which Peking was blatantly advertising to be its major regional foe. Thus, in a statement released by "the secretariat of the Chief of State" (somewhat below the level of an official protest), Cambodia noted "with regret" that "the press under the control

[25] *Komsomolskaya Pravda,* March 19, 1967.
[26] *Ibid.*

of the new authorities in Indonesia has demonstrated increasing hostility toward Cambodia and has increasingly proved to be an instrument of the American warmongers. Indonesia's drift toward an alignment with the enemy . . . may lead to a deterioration of the traditionally friendly relations between Indonesia and Cambodia." [27]

That Peking tends to perceive all its setbacks in international politics as products of U.S.-Soviet collusion rather than antagonism on China's part was illustrated in a *People's Daily* Commentator article which provided considerable insight into Peking's world view. Citing Indonesian, Burmese, and Mongolian opposition to the CPR, Commentator insisted: "But, in reality, the wirepullers behind all these anti-China clowns are just U.S. imperialism and Soviet revisionism alone. The U.S. imperialists and their number one accomplice, the Soviet revisionists, are the engineers and supporters of all anti-China designs and the stage managers of the anti-China farce." Rationalizing the Indonesian leaders' sustained anti-China campaign by citing new U.S. and Soviet aid, Commentator concluded: "Such being the case, it is no wonder that they should so rapidly have opposed China on the orders of their bosses. [But] "this is in fact a good thing. It shows more clearly the distinction between the camp of revolution and the camp of counterrevolution and proves that U.S. imperialism and Soviet revisionism are the headquarters of the world forces of counterrevolution, while the People's Republic of China is a great revolutionary country." [28] Such gross misperception by China of its impact on the international environment does not bode well for any new attempts to reduce its hostility either toward its main antagonists or toward its newly nominated regional foes. That China's adamance may well have the counter effect of pushing countries like Indonesia (and perhaps Burma) into a

[27] Phnom Penh Radio, March 19, 1967.
[28] *People's Daily* Commentator, August 11, 1967.

security arrangement against it has certainly not been acknowledged by Chinese public media. To find a way to
correct the distortion of China's foreign policy information
prism remains a major problem for those having to deal with
the CPR.

INTERNAL INDONESIAN CHANGES
AND THEIR POTENTIAL IMPACT ON CHINA

The Suharto government is attempting to achieve more
than just a change in ruling elites. Through its public policy
pronouncements it seems bent on developing a *regime change*
from the Sukarno period, if by that phrase we mean a change
in the style and direction of Indonesian politics. In part,
such a change, if successful, will have been forced on the
military government by activist elements with which it has
been associated but which are outside its control. Organized
student discontent (KAMI/KAPPI) in the first half of 1966
generated strong momentum not only to ban the PKI but
more significantly to undertake drastic cabinet and economic
reforms and to restore some semblance of pre-Sukarno parliamentary politics. In March 1966, for example, Suharto, with
strong student support, succeeded in obtaining a transfer of
authority from Sukarno, a nationwide ban on the PKI, and
the arrest of fifteen of Sukarno's old Dwikora Cabinet cronies.
Then, as a concession to student and political party demands,
as well as to legitimize the new regime on a separate base
from Sukarno, the military convened a "sanitized" parliament (MPRS) on June 1, purged of PKI and leftist PNI representatives. The MPRS immediately revoked Sukarno's degree authority, designated Suharto as acting president, and
capped the military's banning of the PKI by prohibiting the
dissemination of any form of Marxist ideology.[29]

Suharto's new (Ampera) cabinet appears to be organized

---

[29] Frederick Bunnell, "Indonesia's Quasi-Military Regime," *Current History*,
vol. 52, no. 305 (January, 1967).

on more "Zweckrational" lines with a liberal sprinkling of
pre-Sukarno administrators like the Sultan of Djogjakarta. It
is taking considerable delight in exposing both the corruption of the former regime and its plans for dealing with that
corruption. And for foreign policy purposes it is noteworthy
that the government is blaming much of the economic mismanagement of the Sukarno period on his communist orientation and alliance with the CPR.

Peking provided a running commentary on Suharto's consolidation of power beginning in December 1965, first by
describing the expanded role of such military organs as
KOTI within Sukarno's cabinet and then by juxtaposing this
development with repression of the PKI by the armed
forces.[30] Peking carried a report on Sukarno's attempt to
compromise with the military in February by dropping PKI
leaders from the cabinet in exchange for Nasution's dismissal.[31] By April 1966, after Suharto had created his own
cabinet, *People's Daily* branded its members "right-wing generals and reactionary politicians" who were "trained by former Japanese militarists."[32] When accused by Djakarta
media of interfering in Indonesian affairs, the Peking press
responded that they had been objectively reporting Indonesian developments and for good measure claimed that Nasution's call for general elections to the MPRS was designed
to place it "under the complete control of the right-wing
generals' clique to get rid of once-and-for-all President Sukarno who is now a president only in name."[33]

Although the CPR no longer had any apparent axe to
grind for Sukarno, it condemned Suharto's moves against
the Indonesian president probably in hopes of undermining
the new regime's claim to speak for Indonesia in international relations. Commenting on Suharto's late April re-

[30] NCNA, December 14, 1965.
[31] *Ibid.*, February 23, 1966.
[32] *People's Daily*, April 21, 1966.
[33] *Ibid.*, Commentator and NCNA, April 27, 1966.

organization of the president's Supreme Advisory Council, Peking branded it a play "by strongman Lieut. General Suharto to weaken still another of the president's instruments for ruling" in order to make it an "instrument for dictatorship like the Cooperation Parliament and Provisional People's Consultative Congress." [34] Nasution's call for "the cancellation of Sukarno's title of 'President for life' " was similarly interpreted as a further step in the military's campaign "to get rid of him completely and pave the way for a chieftain of the right-wing general's clique to seize the presidency." [35] Earlier in April, Peking had reported that the military had "restricted Sukarno's freedom of action" and forbade him outside contacts unless specifically approved by Suharto. Thus Chinese media concluded Sukarno was a mere "figurehead," temporarily retained by the army to provide legitimacy for the regime. The convocation of parliament, according to Peking, would serve to "legalize" the coup.[36]

By the summer of 1966, the new Indonesian military leaders were outlining their philosophy of government both for the public at large and for their colleagues to show them the sort of behavior which would be encouraged by the government. Lt. General Panggabean, in an army seminar in Bandung, condemned the "old order" for its lack of democracy: "People were ordered merely to follow their leaders who force-fed them with slogans which were mostly empty. . . . Excessive expectations only fanned the fires of radicalism." By contrast, "the new order which we want to establish is a *Pantjasila* democratic order . . . based on law . . . and sufficient checks and balances. . . . We must strive for depersonalization and promote institutionalization." Denying Sukarno's world view as a basis for successful Indonesian policy, Panggabean insisted: "To be progressive does not

[34] NCNA, April 29, 1966.
[35] *Ibid.*, May 6, 1966.
[36] *Ibid.*, April 9 and 11, 1966.

merely mean to be anti-imperialist, anti-capitalist, anti-this, or anti-that. A social order that is progressive must prove it by its economic progress and social progress." The legitimacy of this new orientation is based on "the decision of the recent fourth session of the MPRS . . . determined democratically and collectively by the highest people's representative body." Panggabean urged the army to return to civic action activities for it is economic stability which "the psychological warfare of the PKI and Gestapu will be aimed precisely at wrecking . . . because the people have never experienced a government which they have been able to trust in economic matters." With considerable foresight, the general concluded that the only way the army could help the government succeed in its task was "to see that a sufficiently large part of its operations produce economic benefits." [37]

These noble appeals by the military favorably contrasted the aims of the Suharto government with the sordid details of the massive corruption that implicated Sukarno, as developed during the trials of Jusuf Dalam and Subandrio. Even more auspicious for the future of popular politics was the passage in November of a Basic Press Bill, which, although outlawing Marxist literature, nonetheless promised that the press "shall have the right to criticize and correct the government . . . and shall not be subject to censorship." [38]

As an outgrowth of the Subandrio-Dalam trials and to pressure Sukarno into surrendering his last semblance of authority to Suharto, the latter submitted a brief to the MPRS in February "containing sufficient proof of President Sukarno's role in periods before, after, and during the Gestapu-PKI coup attempt itself." [39] Less than two weeks later, Sukarno had transferred his remaining executive powers to Suharto, and the latter pointedly responded: "The

[37] See the address at the Second Army Seminar, Bandung, August 25, 1966, as carried by Djakarta Domestic Service, August 25, 1966.
[38] ANTARA, November 12, 1966.
[39] ANTARA, February 11, 1967.

implementation of Bung Karno's policies ran parallel to the PKI's political strategy"—a transparent warning to the Bung that his life was in the hands of the regime and that he had better act accordingly.[40] In hopes of scotching rumors that Sukarno had surrendered his office under duress, the government subsequently issued a long press statement, claiming that the transfer of authority "took place on the initiative of President Sukarno" and that it was by no means a coup but an event "specifically Indonesian in character." As a manifest of its intentions, the government re-emphasized its reliance on the MPRS for popular direction.[41]

Peking's interpretation of the final transfer of authority to Suharto, and MPRS endorsement thereof, was predictably to brand it an "illegal action" which not only deprived Sukarno of his office but also gave the military regime the right to handle "the judicial aspect of the matter affecting Sukarno" —another revelation of the "sinister fascist features of the Indonesian right-wing military group." [42]

The Suharto government has undertaken to implement the 1959 regulation banning Chinese from residing in and conducting commercial operations in rural areas outside provincial capitals. This will not only have a major disruptive effect on the economy by severing long-standing internal trade links but will also obviously exacerbate the Chinese refugee situation and further strain relations with Peking. It seems likely that these moves are calculated by Suharto to force Peking into either breaking relations or suffering continued embarrassment vis-à-vis other Overseas Chinese because of China's inability to protect its nationals abroad. Indeed, a possible explanation for the massive Chinese propaganda campaign in the spring and summer of 1967 against Burma

[40] Djakarta Domestic Service, February 23, 1967. Reports in September 1968 indicated that Sukarno had been placed under house arrest and interrogated concerning his relations with a new clandestine PKI apparatus.
[41] *Ibid.*, February 25, 1967.
[42] NCNA, March 13, 1967.

and Hongkong, particularly, is the felt need to stage a show of support for Overseas Chinese throughout Southeast Asia in order to reassure them of Peking's militant efforts on their behalf and to counteract the obvious débacle to the community in Indonesia. Judging from its propaganda condemnation of "Chiang Kai-shek agents" in the above-mentioned locations, Peking seems particularly exercised over possible changes in allegiance on the part of the Overseas Chinese from the CPR to the KMT on Taiwan. Because of the necessity of continued repatriation of thousands of Chinese still in Indonesia, the CPR cannot afford to break relations totally but instead displaces its ire on the more convenient targets of Hongkong and Macao.

In a public display of wishful thinking, probably designed to buoy the spirits of both its own citizens and the Overseas Chinese, the Peking press declared that the Indonesian military had encountered a grave internal dispute between "the Suharto and Nasution factions" which has "deepened the crisis of their fascist rule." Admitting that the Indonesian Chinese must prepare for "a new anti-China wave" to divert attention from domestic crisis, the press claimed that nevertheless "there is definitely no way out for them." [43] Peking perceives, then, an Indonesian regime committed to long-term hostility toward its own Chinese and the CPR, a regime bent on encouraging American investment and continued Soviet aid and on reviving the private sector of the economy. However, the Indonesian policy change most unacceptable to Peking lies not in the realm of domestic affairs but rather in that of regional orientation. Peking views itself as particularly threatened by what it labels Indonesian moves to create new anti-China alliances in Southeast Asia, allegedly tied to the joint U.S.–Soviet China containment strategy. It is with this dimension that I conclude my analysis.

[43] *People's Daily* Commentator, August 7, 1967.

REGIONAL COOPERATION AND CHINESE XENOPHOBIA

The table in Chapter Six depicting Chinese perceptions of all Indonesian activities in the past-coup period shows that Peking's attention to Indonesian foreign policy comprised its third greatest dimension of concern. Indeed, if all anti-Chinese activities were put into one category, foreign policy would rise to second position. Of the 308 entries, 54 (18 per cent) of the total theme-commentaries were devoted to Indonesia's changed foreign policy orientation. It is noteworthy that this theme did not appear in Chinese media until April 1966, so that during the succeeding fourteen months an average of three commentaries per month dealt with Indonesian foreign affairs, indicating at least moderate salience to Chinese elites. More significant, though not shown in the table, is the fact that the attention trend to Indonesian foreign policy has been rising since June 1966.

An examination of the substance of these commentaries reveals that they are almost entirely concerned with Indonesian moves toward regional reconciliation with Malaysia, its enemy during the Chinese entente; Indonesian attempts to create or to participate in regional groupings composed of pro-Western and nonaligned states, including Japan; and Indonesian moves toward reconciliation with the United States and Great Britain. Needless to say, all of these efforts were perceived negatively by China. A combination of events in mid-1965 seemed virtually to traumatize Peking's foreign policy establishment: Nkrumah's fall in Ghana, the abortion of the Second Afro-Asian Conference, and the unsuccessful coup followed by the PKI's repression and severance of the Sino-Indonesian relationship. Chinese media have since portrayed the CPR as surrounded by enemies, its former allies no longer trustworthy, and complete self-reliance the only way to avoid betrayal.

If this conception of China's desire to avoid cooperative

international contacts is correct, then an examination of its view of Indonesian foreign policy should reveal a sense of betrayal, belligerence, a sellout to China's enemies (including the United States and the Soviet Union), and finally Indonesian attempts to create an alliance against China. Not all of this, it should be stressed, need be considered paranoiac behavior. After all, insofar as Indonesia has displayed the above-mentioned traits, Peking's perception of them is *realistic*, not fantastic. Nevertheless, it is reasonable to speculate that even a partially fanciful perception of Indonesia can reinforce a distorted world view. It is my opinion that such may well be the case with China, for which Indonesia—as either ally or enemy—is a salient foreign policy object.

By September 1966 Chinese media reported Suharto's "intention not only to realize MAPHILINDO, which was once the aim of the United States, but also to drag other neighboring countries into establishing a much bigger federation." The regime was also accused of colluding with Japan and India and of maintaining "secret relations with the Chiang Kai-shek criminals," although at this time Peking did not claim that Indonesia constituted a military threat.[44] Parenthetically, it should be noted that Moscow also viewed Indonesian moves toward regional cooperation as inimical to its interests in Southeast Asia.

In October, Malik declared that Indonesia's new foreign policy would be oriented primarily toward the creation of Southeast Asian cooperation. According to an American analyst, within two months Thailand was circulating, at Indonesia's initiative, a proposal to Malaysia and the Philippines, which suggested the establishment of a new regional association which would combine the ASA and MAPHILINDO.[45] The Indonesian military appeared to be partic-

---

[44] Radio Peking in Indonesian, September 6, 1966.
[45] Bernard K. Gordon, "Foreign Policies in the Wake of Konfrontasi" (paper presented to the Meeting of the Association for Asian Studies, Chicago, March, 1967).

ularly receptive to such an idea insofar as it would help to create Asian anti-communist unity.[46]

Peking's initial recognition of hostile Indonesian military intentions came in a commentary devoted to Djakarta's "economic deals" with Taipei, which were branded initial gambits in a cooperative relationship "to form an offensive semicircle around China from the Sunda Straits to the Taiwan Straits." [47] These Chinese fears were reinforced when, ten days later, Deputy Army Commander Lt. General Panggabean advocated the creation of a joint defense organization in Southeast Asia to face the CPR.[48]

The India-Indonesian joint communiqué in January appeared to associate two of the CPR's major Asian enemies in an antagonistic stance toward China. The communiqué condemned Chinese nuclear testing and stressed that "India and Indonesia held identical views about the danger to world peace from China and Chinese expansionism through military and subversive methods." After suggesting that economic development would prove to be the best method of inhibiting Chinese subversion, Indian Foreign Minister Chagla "assured Indonesia of India's full support to any initiative Indonesia might take to bring about a regional grouping for promoting greater economic cooperation in Southeast Asia." [49] Indicative of its new ties with India and concomitant suspicion of Pakistan (an erstwhile Chinese ally), Djakarta canceled its military assistance agreement with Rawalpindi a week after Chagla's visit.[50]

Peking finally reacted to General Panggabean's appeal for

[46] *Armed Forces Daily Mail* editorial, October 31, 1966, cited in Richard Butwell, "Southeast Asia: How Important—To Whom?" 52, *Current History* (January, 1967): 6.
[47] NCNA, December 13, 1966.
[48] Djakarta Domestic Service, December 24, 1966; and ANTARA, February 27, 1967.
[49] Text of the communiqué in *India News* (Embassy of India to the United States), February 3, 1967, p. 6.
[50] *Ibid.*, February 10, 1967, p. 6.

the creation of an indigenous Southeast Asian security pact in an embassy protest in March. Ignoring the Indonesian military leader's insistence that such an arrangement would help free Southeast Asia from outside influence, the embassy note referred to it as a further step "in hiring yourself out to U.S. imperialism for pay." [51] Taking their cue from this depiction of Panggabean's intentions, Chinese media proceeded to brand subsequent Indonesian efforts at regional organization as new contributions "to Washington's plan for a ring of encirclement of China." [52] As Indonesia's plan for creating a new grouping wider than either ASA or MAPHILINDO seemed to achieve a degree of acceptance by other Southeast Asian states in mid-1967, Peking broadened its propaganda attack from the sole charge of "encirclement against China," adding a warning to potential Indonesian regional allies that Djakarta's motive for any new group was "to realize its own ambition of dominating Southeast Asia." Peking pointed to Cambodia as the example for other states to emulate—Cambodia whose "Foreign Ministry declared . . . that it would definitely not join the organization" whose purpose "was to serve U.S. neocolonialism." [53] That the CPR views apprehensively the possibility of a broad-gauged cooperative enterprise including Indonesia, Thailand, Malaysia, the Philippines, South Vietnam, and even Laos, Burma, and Cambodia linking up with India was evidenced by its treatment of Indian Foreign Minister Chagla's May visit to Malaya and Singapore. During the course of his visit, Chagla referred to an Asian Council and Common Market embracing the states mentioned above together with Japan and Australia. Such a grouping, the realization of which is highly unlikely, was immediately opposed by Peking as India's way to "assist the

[51] CPR embassy note carried by NCNA, March 7, 1967.
[52] NCNA, March 30, 1967, and April 13, 1967, and *People's Daily* editorial, April 27 1967.
[53] NCNA, May 13, 1967.

smaller alliance plotted by the Indonesian reactionaries."
Dismissing Indonesian, Indian, and Malaysian attestations
that any new organization would serve exclusively economic
and cultural ends, Peking reiterated its charge that U.S. imperialism was behind these machinations to achieve "its
sinister aim of opposing China, but uses the name of 'economic cooperation' to evade condemnation by world public
opinion." [54] Undoubtedly reinforcing Peking's view of Indonesia's belligerent regional intentions, General Panggabean
was appointed Acting Army Commander in late May, a position which may have provided him with considerable policy
influence in the cabinet in general and the upper ranks of
the military in particular.[55] Equally important, to Peking it
probably appeared that Suharto was endorsing Panggabean's
notion of a regional security arrangement directed explicitly
against China by rewarding him with the top army post.

It seemed that Peking's concern was, in part, justified in
August when "a new anti-China, anticommunist alliance was
knocked together on orders of U.S. imperialism in Bangkok
. . . under the name 'Association of Southeast Asian Nations' " for which "the Suharto-Nasution Fascist Military Regime of Indonesia has worked slavishly for more than six
months." Composed of Indonesia, the Philippines, Thailand,
Malaysia, and Singapore, the new grouping amalgamates the
former ASA and MAPHILINDO and, like them, purports
to be concerned with social, economic, and cultural affairs.
China branded this "nothing but a lie" to mask its real
purpose of cooperating with "existing international and
regional organizations which oppose China and oppose communism," and hence, she said, it may be called "the twin
brother of SEATO." China's only apparent consolation was
Cambodia's reiterated refusal to join.[56]

[54] *Ibid.*, May 16, 1967.
[55] Djakarta Domestic Service, May 29, 1967.
[56] NCNA, August 9, 1967.

Cataloging its complaints against Suharto in a lengthy commentary, Peking underlined its perception of the regime's association with the United States and the "accomplices of U.S. imperialism in Asia, such as Thailand, the Philippines, Japan, and India." Now, the commentary protested, Indonesia is even sending its military to America for training again and is receiving both U.S. and Soviet support in its plans for "rigging up a military alliance against communism and China." [57]

Peking's apparent misperception of the goals of the new Association of Southeast Asian Nations (ASEAN) and the Asia and Pacific Council may not be as distorted as it first appears. As Bernard Gordon points out, a grouping as broad as the former could provide a cooperatively inclined, anticommunist Indonesia with the framework it needs for a grand foreign policy role in Asia.[58] ASEAN, for example, could significantly contribute to Indonesian economic development by providing guaranteed markets, and, as Peking has charged, could also serve as part of a strategic periphery around the mainland which could be linked up with India on the south and Japan on the north. Such a prospect is hardly auspicious for the CPR. Peking's opposition to organizational efforts by noncommunist Asian states, even for exclusively economic ends, appears reasonable, for such organizations might have "spillover" effects into other functional areas including the military. In any case, China's primary threat to the region lies less in traditional military assault as practiced in the Korean War and more in potential subversion as illustrated by Chinese policy in Vietnam and Thailand. Successful regional cooperation, insofar as it contributes to *national* development, could blunt the sharp edge of China's revolutionary ideology insofar as economic growth is in-

---

[57] *Ibid.,* June 23, 1967.
[58] Bernard K. Gordon, "Regionalism and Instability in Southeast Asia," 10, no. 2, *Orbis* (Summer, 1966), 454.

versely proportional to internal alienation. Thus, Peking would have fewer target groups within any given state to employ against either the government, as in South Vietnam and Thailand, or anticommunist elites, as in Indonesia. Indeed, even the Soviet Union, while deploring the creation of ASEAN as much as the CPR did, declared that Peking had brought it on itself.[59]

Despite the above analysis of a possible trend toward Indonesian anti-communist regional cooperation and Peking's objections, the likelihood of such a scenario has yet to be established. Southeast Asian cooperation remains minimal and Indonesia's role within it suspect. Peking and Djakarta have begun a *propaganda war* as common values have been metamorphosed into conflicting ones. However, because conflicting interests have not attained the same intensity level as conflicting values, hostilities between the two states have been confined primarily to the propaganda level; that is, the techniques of conflict have been verbal rather than action oriented. Action conflict has been more or less restricted to such symbolic deeds as the storming of each other's diplomatic establishments, a favorite technique of both states even before they became antagonists. Largely because of geographical distance, the Sino-Indonesian conflict has remained essentially verbal, because although value conflict is high, interest conflict is still relatively low. That is, neither has the ability to subvert the other nor effectively to challenge the other's major foreign policy goals. Thus, the techniques of conflict employed are relatively modest. A scalor representation comparing the Sino-Indonesian relationship in the pre- and post-coup periods would look something like this.

Note that the range between X and Y is less for the Interest Distribution and Technique Intensity Scales than the other two more general measurements of relationship because of the positive correlation between intensity of conflicting in-

RELATIONSHIP SCALE BETWEEN CHINA AND INDONESIA
IN THE PRE- AND POST-COUP PERIODS

X = Pre-Coup
Y = Post-Coup

I–*Interest Distribution Scale*

Common Interests	100%	X	75%	50%		25%		0%	
	0%		25%	50%	Y	75%		100%	Conflicting Interests

II–*Amity/Enmity Scale*

Amity	100%	X	75%	50%		25%		0%	
	0%		25%	50%		75%	Y	100%	Enmity

III–*Collaboration/Conflict Scale*

Collaboration	100%	X	75%	50%		25%		0%	
	0%		25%	50%		75%	Y	100%	Conflict

IV–*Technique Intensity Scale*

Collaboration Technique	100%	X	75%	50%		25%		0%	
	0%		25%	50%	Y	75%		100%	Conflict Techniques

Adapted from Andrew M. Scott, *The Functioning of the International Political System* (New York: Macmillan Company, 1967), p. 148.

terests and number and kinds of techniques employed in the conflict.

*   *   *

There is no neat conclusion to an extended analysis of the changing relationship between China and Indonesia. If anything, this study has underlined how mercurial relations between states can be even among those considered staunchest allies when elites and values change. We have focused on only one aspect of foreign policy analysis—national perceptions—to the exclusion of decision-making, negotiation, and deterrence theory, all of which should be applied for a more complete picture of the Sino-Indonesian case. Nevertheless, of all these conceptual frameworks, a strong case can be made for the precedence of perceptual analysis, insofar as it is the decision-makers' perceptions of their environment which help to determine the range of strategies available for dealing with it. For example, in the pre-coup period, because it perceived Sukarno to be an ally, the CCP encouraged the PKI's open participation in the Indonesian political process despite the former's ideological antipathy to the party's subordination within a noncommunist popular front. Thus, Chinese leaders temporarily excluded the subversion option from their range of strategies in dealing with Indonesia. Similarly, in the post-coup period, because of China's overarching concern with what it pictures as Soviet-American collusion against her, Peking has fitted its break with Indonesia into the broader perceptual orientation that all states opposing China must *ipso facto* be tools of a Soviet-American conspiracy. It seems reasonable to speculate that such a rigid perceptual pattern forecloses avenues of approach to a number of states whose relations with China might be meliorated on a bilateral basis, such as Indonesia and, more recently, Burma.

For students of international politics and Chinese foreign policy, it is my hope that this analysis of Chinese perceptions of the changing relations with Indonesia has yielded some insight into how Chinese documentary material may be ordered and analyzed, as well as into the peculiar dynamics of Chinese foreign policy perceptions and style in the 1960's as China moves toward the status of a major world power. As this study has attempted to show, China is still plagued by xenophobia and a national superiority complex, both of which distort its view of the intentions of others and help to promote grandiose plans. The key question for the future is whether Chinese leaders can learn and accept the norms of pacific international politics as they acquire thermonuclear capability (much as the Soviet leaders have so learned) and modify their views of an inveterately hostile environment, or whether they will employ their new military instruments to carve out a sphere of hegemony in Asia, perhaps even precipitating the holocaust that the Soviet Union and the United States have managed to avoid. In any event, continued close analysis of China's views of its allies and enemies remains the best technique available for predicting the range of policy options Chinese leaders are likely to consider.

Selected Glossary of Indonesian Names, Abbreviations, and Acronyms

ABRI	–The Army
ASA	–Association of Southeast Asia, composed of Malaysia, Thailand, and the Philippines; set up in 1961
ASEAN	–Association of Southeast Asian Nations, successor to both ASA and MAPHILINDO; created in August 1967
Baperki	–Indonesian Overseas Chinese Association, heavily dependent on PKI
Barisan Sosialis	–Crypto-communist party in Singapore
BTI	–PKI-controlled Indonesian Peasants' Association
Gerwani	–PKI-controlled Indonesian Women's Organization
Gestapu	–The September 30 Movement, the name given to the abortive leftist Indonesian coup attempt
KAMI/KAPPI	–Anticommunist college and high-school student movement created in the wake of Gestapu
KOTI	–Supreme Operations Command, the highest military-civilian executive body under Sukarno

Konfrontasi	–Indonesia's policy of opposing the formation of Malaysia, initiated in 1963
KOTRAR	–Supreme Command for Retooling the Apparatus of the Revolution on which the PKI obtained some representation
Mahmilub	–The military tribunal created by the Suharto government to adjudicate the cases of those accused of involvement in Gestapu
MAINEKIBU	–Cultural Manifesto of 1964 composed by liberal intellectuals in an attempt to weaken the PKI's political position
MAPHILINDO	–Association of Malaysia, Philippines, and Indonesia formed in 1962
MANIPOL	–Political Manifesto, title of Sukarno's 1959 Independence Day Speech, considered a basic document of his regime
MPRS	–The Indonesian Cooperation Parliament
Marhaen	–A term for the masses of the population
Masjumi	–A liberal Moslem party outlawed because of its implication in the 1957–59 Outer Islands Rebellion
Murba	–National Marxist Party, a rival to the PKI
NASAKOM	–The combination of nationalist, religious, and communist components proposed by the PKI for a Sukarno Cabinet.
Nawaksara	–Sukarno's speech of January 10, 1967, in which he tried to absolve himself of any blame for Gestapu
Nekolim	–Sukarno's acronym for neocolonialism-imperialism
NU	–Islamic Political party during Sukarno's regime
Pantjasila	–Five Principles of the Indonesian state: nationalism, social justice, democracy, internationalism, belief in God
Partindo	–Minor leftist political party

Pemuda Rakjat –PKI youth organization

Perti   –Minor PKI-oriented political party

PNI   –Indonesian Nationalist Party; during Sukarno
                era, the largest party in Indonesia

PSI   –The democratic Indonesian Socialist Party, out-
                lawed because of its implication in the 1957–59
                Outer Islands Rebellion

SOBSI   –PKI-controlled trade union federation, largest
                in Indonesia

TAVIP   –Title of President Sukarno's Independence Day
                Address, 1964.

Index

Abdul Rahman, 43
Afro-Asian Conference, 20, 26, 51, 61, 63–65, 194
Afro-Asian Journalists' Association, 147, 149–50
Afro-Asian Peoples Solidarity Organization, 12, 20, 148
Agrarian Law of 1960, 83–85, 93, 104
Aidit, D. N., 34, 38–39, 41, 65, 75–110, 114, 119, 152–54, 156–58, 162–63, 166
Alker, Hayward, 4
ASEAN, 198–99
Asian Games, 28, 51
Association of Southeast Asia (ASA), 195–98
Astrawinata, 92
Azahari, 33–35, 178

Bandung Conference, 23, 58
Bangkok talks (1964), 42; (1966), 179
Banks, Arthur, 5
Baperki, 94, 114
Barisan Sosialis, 34

Belgrade Conference (1961), 19, 26, 49
Bobrow, Davis B., 4
Body for the Promotion of Sukarnoism (BPS), 95, 97, 105
Brunei, 32–33
BTI, 42, 82–85, 92, 97, 103, 104, 174

Chen I, 27, 43, 62–63, 69, 107, 143, 158
China: on arming PKI, 104–8, 114; and entente with Indonesia, 13–29, 73, 116–18, 157; and foreign policy development, 16–21, 37–48, 53, 56, 70, 146–50, 199–203; and Great Cultural Revolution, 162, 168, 171–72, 175, 177; and the Indonesian coup, 111–50, 162–75; and the Japan and Korean communist parties, 169; and perceptions of environment, 13–15, 69, 125–30, 169–70, 176–78, 181, 187, 193–203; and Singapore, 47; Sino-Soviet polemic, 18–21, 35, 39, 57, 59, 61, 63, 71, 79–81, 120, 122–23, 149, 157–59,

THE JOHNS HOPKINS PRESS

Designed by Arlene J. Sheer

Composed in Linotype Baskerville text and Baskerville Bold display
by The Colonial Press Inc.

Printed offset by The Colonial Press Inc.
on 60-lb. Warren Old Style Wove

Bound by The Colonial Press Inc.
in Columbia Riverside Vellum